Google Search
Secrets

Neal-Schuman purchases fund advocacy, awareness, and accreditation programs for library professionals worldwide.

Google Search Secrets

Christa Burns and Michael P. Sauers

Neal-Schuman

An imprint of the American Library Association

CHICAGO 2014

Christa Burns is the Special Projects Librarian, Technology and Access Services, at the Nebraska Library Commission. She provides organization, training, and consultation for special projects, such as the Gates Foundation grants for libraries, E-rate, Learning 2.0, and group purchases of library products and services. Christa also coordinates, produces, and hosts the Commission's weekly webinar series, NCompass Live. Before coming to Nebraska in 2000, Christa spent more than eight years at Pace University in Westchester County, NY, starting as a Reference Librarian and working her way up to become Head of Research and Information Services. She received her MLS from the University of Albany School of Information Science and Policy in 1991, and her BA from the University of Binghamton in English Literature and Folklore. In her spare time, Christa is a gamer, bibliophile, floriculturist, amateur chef, and ferret and cat minion.

Michael Sauers is currently the Technology Innovation Librarian for the Nebraska Library Commission in Lincoln, Nebraska, and has been training librarians in technology for almost 20 years. He has been a public library trustee, a bookstore manager for a library Friends group, a reference librarian, serials cataloger, technology consultant, and bookseller. He earned his MLS in 1995 from the University at Albany's School of Information Science and Policy. He blogs at travelinlibrarian.info, runs Web sites for authors and historical societies, takes many, many photos, and reads more than 100 books a year. This is Michael's twelfth book.

© 2014 by the American Library Association.

Printed in the United States of America
18 17 16 15 14   5 4 3 2 1

Extensive effort has gone into ensuring the reliability of the information in this book; however, the publisher makes no warranty, express or implied, with respect to the material contained herein.

ISBNs: 978-1-55570-923-5 (paper); 978-1-55570-971-6 (PDF). For more information on digital formats, visit the ALA Store at alastore.ala.org and select eEditions.

Library of Congress Cataloging-in-Publication Data

Burns, Christa.
   Google search secrets / Christa Burns and Michael P. Sauers.
     pages   cm
   Includes bibliographical references and index.
   ISBN 978-1-55570-923-5 (alk. paper)
   1. Google. 2. Web search engines. 3. Web applications. 4. Database
   searching. I. Sauers, Michael P. II. Title.
ZA4234.G64B87 2014
025.04252—dc23
                       2013016976

Book design by Kimberly Thornton in Helvetica Neue, Popular, and Charis SIL.

♾ This paper meets the requirements of ANSI/NISO Z39.48-1992 (Permanence of Paper).

For Cordwainer Bird
—*Michael*

For John. He knows why.
—*Christa*

contents

introduction

> Google's mission is to organize the world's information
> and make it universally accessible and useful.
>
> —*Google's mission statement (http://www.google.com/about/company)*

I f you're a librarian reading this (or not) you may remember a time when we didn't have Google to help us find what we were looking for. From a perspective of a new librarian working a reference desk, those times probably seem like the dark ages. A time when we had to walk from one end of the building to another, find the right book, consult an index, and hope the volume contained the needed information. Granted, we still do that, but not nearly as often as we used to.

If you're not a librarian, please don't think that Google will answer all your questions. Trust us—we know this for a fact.

Regardless of all this, chances are you're a daily Google user. As Michael's step daughters are fond of saying, "Just ask the almighty Google machine." Google isn't just a company name, it's a verb. How's that for having an impact?

In 2008 Michael wrote, and Neal-Schuman published, *Searching 2.0*, a guide to searching not only some of Google's (then) lesser-known interfaces, but many other search engines that gave us access to the new types of information available online. In 2011, he was asked to write a follow-up and suggested that maybe this time he would be willing, with Christa's help, to focus just on Google. You're holding the result in your hands right now.

Google has fingers in many different pies, from cars to computer operating systems. But at its heart is search, and search is what we've focused on in this book.

In chapter 1 we take you through a brief history of Google and talk about some of those other pies we just mentioned. The bulk of chapter 1, however, covers the common features of Google search that apply across the rest of the search services covered in this book.

Chapter 2 dives into Google's web search, the default search interface that is found at google.com. Here we introduce Google Search's general look and feel and how web results are presented, along with your first set of search filters for narrowing your results.

From this point forward chapters 3 through 10 all follow the same pattern of introducing you to a different search interface that focuses results on a different type of information. From there we cover the basic and advanced search interfaces, the results, and search filters for each of the topics covered by that search. These chapters cover Google Images, Google News, Google Videos, Google Maps, Google Blog Search, Google Scholar, Google Patents, and Google Books accordingly.

With chapter 11 we take a slightly different approach and introduce you to the Google Alerts service. Simply put, Google Alerts allows you to automate your searching and have the results delivered to you automatically. If you're someone who searches for new content on a single subject with any regularity, this is the chapter for you.

Finally, in chapter 12, we end with what are known as search features. Hidden within Google are many different search types that won't just find a page on the web that has your answer, but will give you the answer directly. Here we cover those types of searches.

You don't necessarily need to read these chapters in order, but we highly recommend that you at least read chapter 1 first since that will cover a lot of common material that applies to the rest of the chapters in the book.

Naturally, Google services and features are constantly evolving. To assist you in keeping up with the changing world of Google, we have set up a website where we will be posting updates after the publication of this book (http:// googlesearchsecretsbook.blogspot.com).

One last note: even though the writing of the chapters in this book were evenly divided between us, we decided not to specify who wrote which. Therefore we decided to phrase most of the text in the first-person plural unless specifically referring to something one of us has done outside of this book. In those cases we referred to ourselves in the third person.

chapter 1

Welcome to Google

It's Google's world; we're just living in it.

THAT'S NOT ENTIRELY true, but it can oftentimes feel that way. With products and services and research and innovation, Google has ingrained itself into many parts of our lives. And it's likely to remain that way for the foreseeable future. Google's mission is "to organize the world's information and make it universally accessible and useful." With all the different ways that Google has developed to search the Internet, this is becoming closer to reality. Harnessing this accessibility and usefulness via Google's various search options is the purpose of our book.

A Very Brief History of Google

Google was born in 1996. Originally called BackRub, it was the creation of Stanford University students Larry Page and Sergey Brin as a better way to organize and search the growing web. Rather than ranking results by counting how many times search terms appeared on a page, as other search engines at the time did, they created a search engine that determined a website's relevance by counting the number of pages, and the importance of those pages, that linked back to the original site.[1]

Before incorporating in 1998, the name was changed to Google, a misspelling of *googol*, the mathematical term for a 1 followed by one hundred 0s.

It was chosen as the new name to reflect their desire to index the immense amount of data on the Internet. Since its incorporation, Google has expanded its offerings beyond the original search engine. The company has developed its own products and has acquired other products, further expanding the Google empire.

Other Google Products and Services

This book will focus on searching Google, but there's much more that Google does. Here are just a few examples.

- *Android*
  Linux-based operating system for mobile devices such as smartphones and tablet computers. http://www.android.com

- *Gmail*
  Free webmail IMAP and POP e-mail service provided by Google, known for its abundant storage, intuitive search-based interface and elasticity. It was first released in an invitation-only form on April 1, 2004. http://mail.google.com

- *Google Chrome and Google Chrome OS/Chromebook*
  Google Chrome is Google's web browser and Chrome OS is a computer operating system based on the Chrome browser. In a few cases we'll be mentioning Google search features that are only available if you're using one of these platforms. (Don't worry, it's just one or two items.) http://www.google.com/chrome and http://www.google.com/chromebook

- *Google Glass*
  Head-mounted wearable computer, similar to eyeglasses but with a heads-up display instead of traditional lenses. www.google.com/glass

- *Google Driverless Car*
  Experimental project that involves developing technology for driverless cars. The system combines information gathered from Google Street View with artificial intelligence software that combines input from video cameras inside the car and sensors on the outside. http://en.wikipedia.org/wiki/Google_driverless_car

Common Search Elements

A note before we get started: unless otherwise stated, for all of our examples you do not need to be logged into a Google account.

There are some features of Google searching that apply to all the different search interfaces we'll be covering. Features specific to a type of search will be covered in the relevant chapter.

- *Autocomplete*
  As you type within the search box on Google, the autocomplete algorithm offers searches that might be similar to the one you're typing. The algorithm predicts and displays search queries based on other users' search activities and the contents of web pages indexed by Google (figure 1.1).

Figure 1.1 Autocomplete example

- *Search as you type*
  In 2010, Google introduced Google Instant, a search enhancement that shows results as you type. As soon as you start typing your search terms into the search box, Google brings up possible results based upon the first letters you type, as shown in figure 1.2. As you type more, the results will change to match what you've now typed. Once you see results that match what you need, you can stop typing and start browsing your results. Basically, Google Instant speeds up your search time and gets you your results a few seconds quicker. If you don't want to use Google Instant, you can turn it off. After you have your search results, click the gear icon in the upper right corner of the results and choose "Search Settings." You can choose to show Google Instant predictions "only when your computer is fast enough," "always show Instant results," or "never show Instant results."

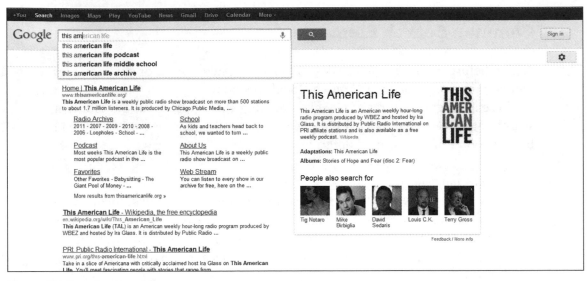

Figure 1.2 Search as you type

- *Voice search*
  With an attached microphone, you can speak your search, rather than typing it. Click the mic icon in the Google Chrome search bar and start talking (figure 1.3). This is one of those features that's available only when you're using the Google Chrome browser.

- *Next/Previous page*
  If the web page or information you're looking for is not on the first page of search results, you can click "Next" at the bottom of the page to see more results (figure 1.4). Remember, the further into the results pages you get, the less relevant the results may become.

Figure 1.3 Speak your search in Chrome

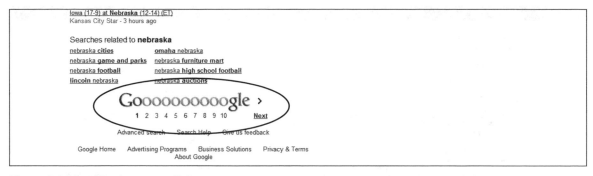

Figure 1.4 Next/Previous page links

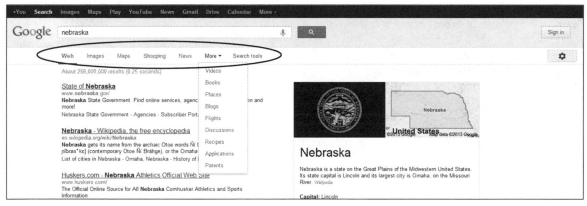

Figure 1.5 Search by result type links

- *Result types*
  You can limit your search results to a particular type of content on the top above your search results: Web, Images, Maps, Shipping, Books, and so on. Click "More" to see additional types (figure 1.5).

- *Searching Google+*
  In the past you would use a + before a keyword word to require it. Today, all keywords are automatically considered required. Only use a + sign when you want to search for content within Google+ (figure 1.6).

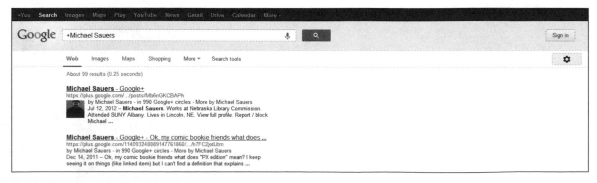

Figure 1.6 A search for *+Michael Sauers*

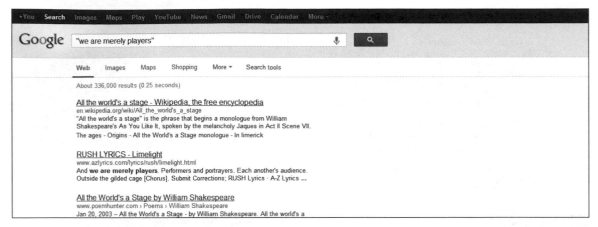

Figure 1.7 Example of exact phrase search results

- *Quotes for phrases*
  To search for an exact phrase, put it in quotes (figure 1.7).

- *Capitalization*
  Capitalization doesn't matter; *This* is the same as *ThiS*.

- *Special characters*
  Most special characters are ignored; ©, for example.

- *Word order*
  To increase the relevance of search results, Google does pay attention to the order in which you enter your search terms. The difference is shown in figures 1.8 and 1.9.

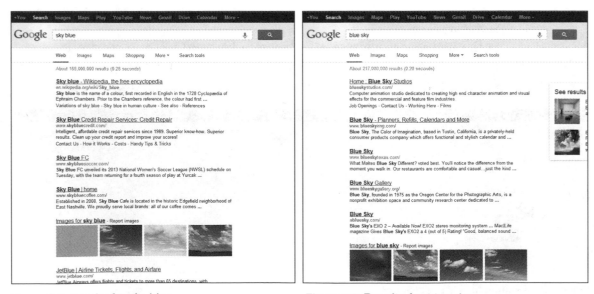

Figure 1.8 Results for *sky blue*   *Figure 1.9* Results for *blue sky*

SEARCH OPERATORS

Google search operators can be used to focus your search. Here we will detail the common operators. In each of the following chapters, you will learn the operators specific to that chapter's type of searching. All these options are available to you when you do your basic search, but you need to know the syntax necessary to access them. If you go to an Advanced Search screen, you just fill out the fields you wish to use and click the "Advanced Search" button.

The first section of an Advanced Search form, "Find pages with . . . ," is designed to find web pages that have the following:

- *All these words*
  This field works as a Boolean "AND." Every word in this field will be considered in the search.

- *This exact word or phrase*
  This field is used in place of the standard quotation marks to form a phrase. All words in this field will be considered in the order given.

- *Any of these words*
  This field works as a Boolean "OR." Any word in this field will be considered in the search, but only any one word of the list need be considered.

- *None of these words*
  This field works as a Boolean "NOT" (AND NOT). Words in this field will be explicitly excluded from consideration in the results list.

- *Numbers ranging from*
  Separate numbers by two periods (with no spaces) to see results that contain numbers in a given range of things like dates, prices, and measurements. For example, if you're looking for reviews of digital cameras costing between $200 and $300, you could enter those values here.

You may have noticed that our wording is not exactly standard when it comes to explaining these items. Typically when describing a Boolean operator, such as "AND," one would say that both words "must appear in the result." However, based on how Google's search algorithm works, at times you can require a word to be present—but that word will not appear in the result. Therefore, we needed to say that the words "will be considered in the search," as opposed to the more standard "must appear" language.

More Search Options

The final section on the Advanced Search page, "You can also . . . ," has links to other search types, which work independently of one another and anything else you may do on this page.

FIND PAGES THAT ARE SIMILAR TO, OR LINK TO, A URL

You can use special search operators to find pages that are similar to or link to a specific URL. For example, let's say we're looking for the websites of other libraries in our area. We know that the URL for our home library is http://www.lincolnlibraries.org/, so we use the "related" operator and enter *related:lincolnlibraries.org* into the Google search box, and receive the results shown in figure 1.10.

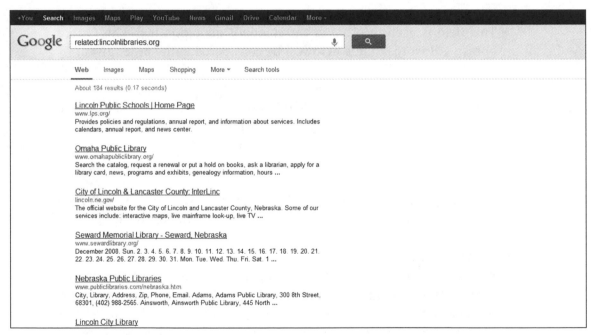

Figure 1.10 Similar pages search for *lincolnlibraries.org*

As you can see from the results, we've been presented with a list of other libraries and library-like institutions in Nebraska and surrounding states. The list is not geographically limited, but generally the farther down the list we go, the farther out into the rest of the state the libraries are located.

The "link:" operator gives you a list of results to pages linked to the URL that you entered. For example, if we'd like to know what websites link back to a particular site, we would enter *link:nlc.nebraska.gov* into the Google search box. Figure 1.11 shows the results.

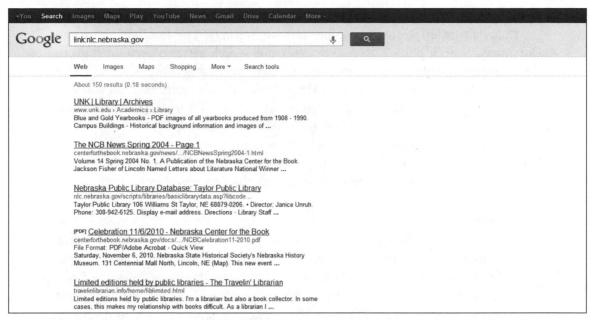

Figure 1.11 **Pages that link to *nlc.nebraska.gov***

Be aware that the "link:" operator will search only for pages that link to the exact URL that you enter. Thus, for the previous example, you will get results that link only to that web page but not to any other page on that website. To see links to any other page on the site, you would use *link:nlc.nebraska.gov/ncompasslive*, for example.

You can also "Search pages you've visited," if you are logged into your Google account. Since that is not something that you would generally do when helping your patrons, we do not cover that option in this book.

If the Advanced Search options aren't finding what you need, you can "Use operators in the search box." This is a more complex way of doing most of the searches that are available to you on the Advanced Search page. There is a list of these, with examples, from this link at the bottom of the Advanced Search page.

Search Settings

The Search Settings page is where you can customize your preferences in Google search. Changing any of these settings means you are changing them indefinitely for the computer you are using. So, if you are on a computer that is used by more than one person, you may want to consider your changes carefully. By signing in to Google, you can have these settings affect your own account as opposed to the particular computer. To reinstate your customized settings, just log in to your Google account.

There are multiple access points to your settings. The last option on the Advanced Search page is to "Customize your search settings"; you can go to http://www.google.com/preferences, or after you have done a search, you can click the gear icon in the upper right corner of the results page and choose "Search settings." To finalize any changes you make on these screens, click on the "Save" button at the bottom of the screen.

On the left side of the screen, you will see that there are three categories on the Search Settings page (figure 1.12): Search results, Languages, and Location. In the Search results category, you have the following options:

- *SafeSearch filters*
  SafeSearch is Google's technology for filtering out potentially offensive content. This option allows you to change your browser settings to help eliminate adult content from your search results. By default, the Safe-Search filter is disabled. To enable SafeSearch, click the "Filter explicit results" check box. This will filter sexually explicit video and images from Google Search result pages, as well as results that might link to explicit content. To disable the SafeSearch filter, uncheck the "Filter explicit results" option. Please be aware that no filter is perfect. Even Google says that "we do our best to keep SafeSearch as up-to-date and

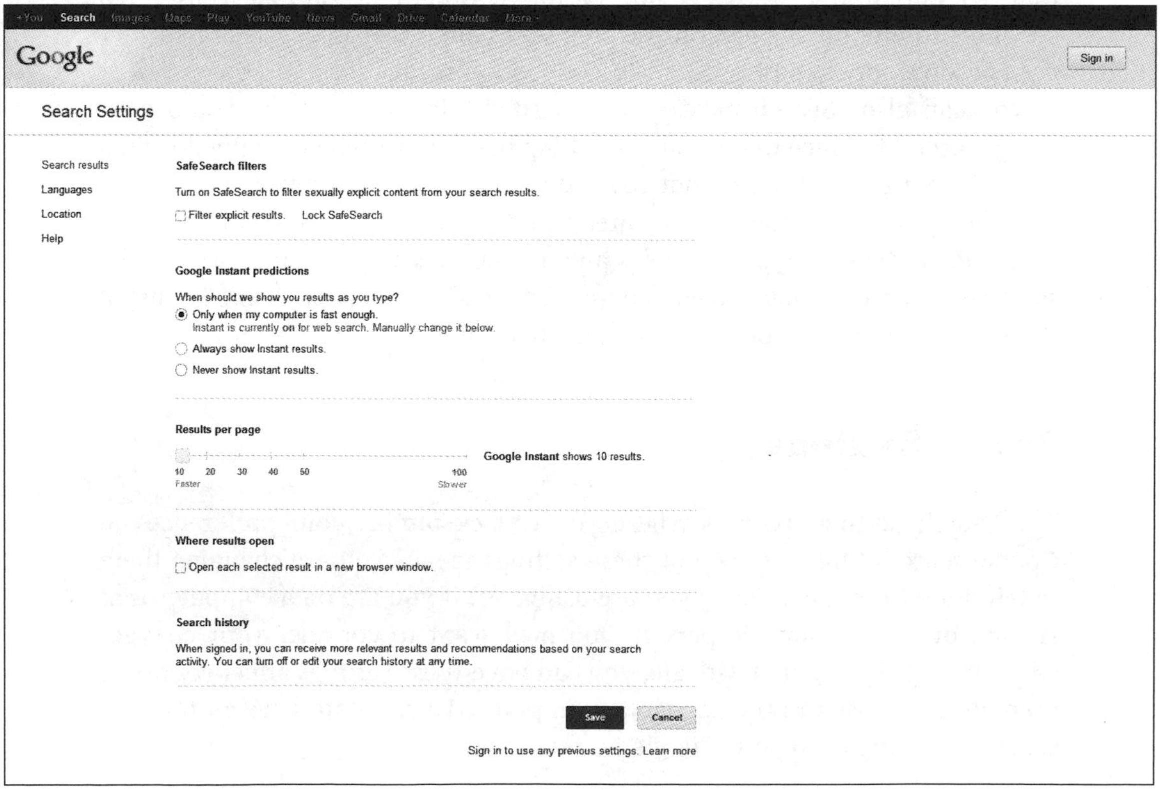

Figure 1.12 Google's Search Settings page

comprehensive as possible, but inappropriate sites will sometimes slip through the cracks." Also, this is not a replacement for any filtering software you may be considering installing in your library. Anyone can easily get around this filter by coming back to this page and changing the setting.

- *Google Instant predictions*
  Also discussed earlier in this chapter, this is where you can choose to show Google Instant predictions "only when your computer is fast enough," "always show Instant results," or "never show Instant results."

- *Results per page*
  Here you can set how many results you would like per screen. The default is 10, but if you would like more, you can change this to 20, 30, 40, 50, or 100.

- *Where results open*
  When this option is selected, the result you click on will be opened in a new window or tab (if your browser supports tabbed browsing). This will allow you to open multiple results at the same time instead of having to move back and forth between results and the Google results list. If you are not comfortable working with multiple browser windows or tabs, checking this option is not recommended.

- The final two options, blocking unwanted results and web history, are available only when you are logged in to your Google account, and thus will not be covered in this book.

The second category on the Search Settings page is Languages (figure 1.13).

- *For Google text*
  Here you may choose whichever of the available languages you wish to use for Google's interface. Choosing an option here will "permanently" change Google's interface for your computer. From this point forward (until you change it again), when you go to www.google.com, you will be presented with the language you've selected.

- *For Search results*
  The default setting for Google's search language is "Search for pages written in any language." This instructs Google to retrieve all relevant results regardless of the language the result is written in. By changing this setting to "Prefer pages written in these language(s):" you can then select one or more of the 46 languages listed to limit your results. Here

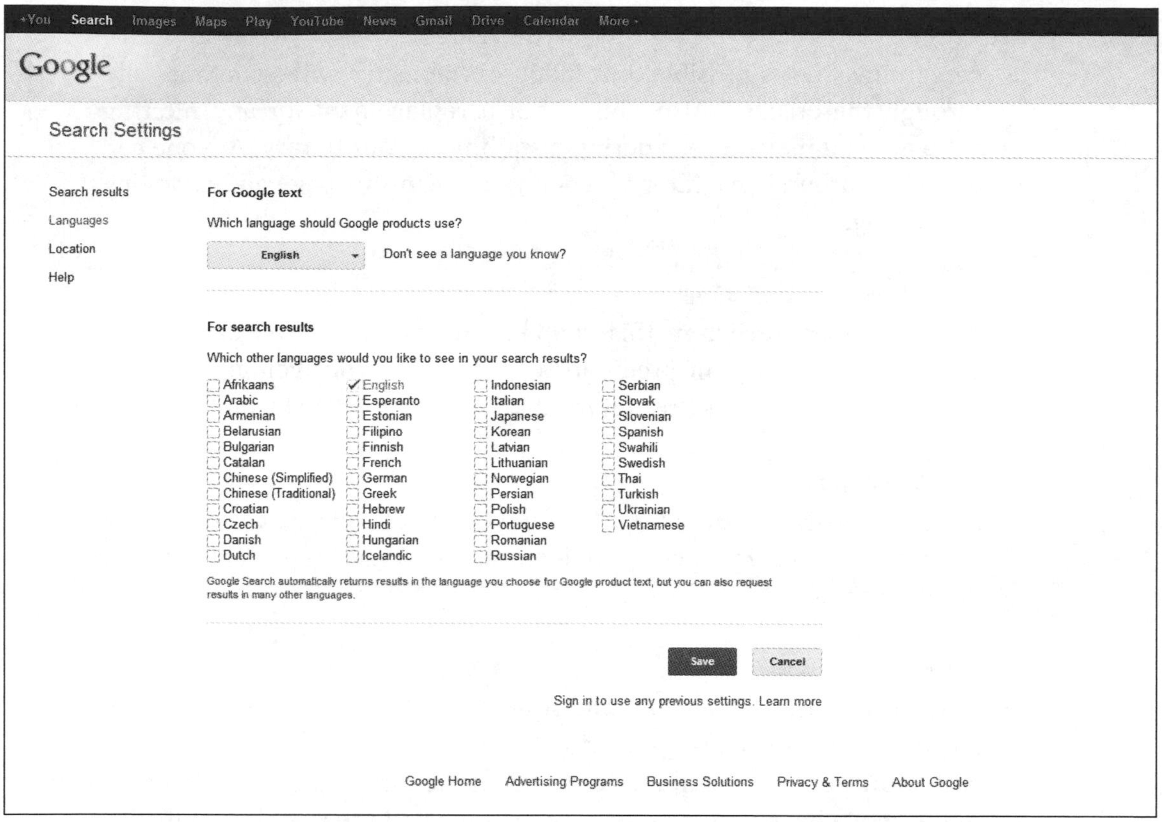

Figure 1.13 Google's Languages Settings page

you can limit your results to more than one language. However, you must remember that by choosing this option, Google will remember this limitation until you come back and change it again.

The last category on the Search Settings page is Location (figure 1.14). This is where you can chose the location you would like Google to use for Google Search, Google Maps, and other Google products. You can enter a street

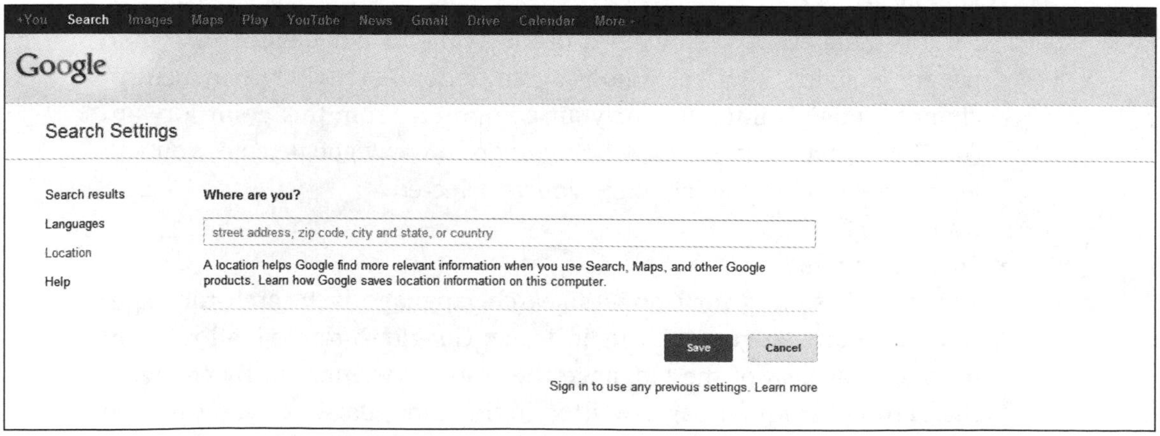

Figure 1.14 Google's Location Setting page

address, zip code, city and state, or country. By default, Google's location detection technology will automatically set a location for you using your IP address, but you can change that location to anyplace you like and then save it as your default location.

So, now that we've got the common items covered, let's get a little more specific and start searching.

NOTE

1. This is a bit of a simplification of how Google's "Page Rank" works, as today Google determines relevancy using literally hundreds of factors. However, it's a good enough explanation for our purposes.

chapter 2

Google
Web Search

THIS CHAPTER PRESENTS an overview of the basic Google Web Search, focusing on the major features to show how you can use them in your daily reference work.

Google's central purpose is to search the whole web—as much as it can possibly index, anyway. There are also ways to search subsections of the web or certain types of material. For each of these services, we do not cover all the available features here. In some cases, we cover topics in later chapters. In other cases, because some features may not be as useful at the reference desk, we focus on only the most useful features of these services.

Basic Search

Nearly every Internet user today is familiar with the Google home page. But, just as a reminder, here it is again in figure 2.1.

Figure 2.1 The Google home page

By default, any search performed from this page will search Google's database of web content. From here you can also click on links to search various other Google databases, such as Images, Videos, News, Books, and Maps. Others are available through the "More" link, which we cover later in this chapter. Google also offers users the ability to customize their Google home page through the "Sign in" to their Google account at the upper right corner of the page.

Basic searches are performed by entering your search terms, and any operators as needed, into the search box and clicking on one of the two available buttons. Those buttons are "Google Search" and "I'm Feeling Lucky." Clicking on the "Google Search" button—which can also be activated by pressing your Enter key while your cursor is in the search box—performs your search and presents you with a list of results. Clicking on "I'm Feeling Lucky" performs your search, but instead of presenting you with a list of results, it takes you right to the page that was the first result. This is as if you had clicked on "Google Search," retrieved your list of results, and clicked on the first result yourself.

The "I'm Feeling Lucky" option works very well when you're pretty sure of where you're going to end up. For example, searching on such terms as *microsoft*, *nike*, or *wikipedia* will retrieve for you www.microsoft.com, www.nike.com, and www.wikipedia.org, respectively. However, if you're not sure of the end result, as with more complex searches, or if you don't want to take the chance of displaying something potentially inappropriate to a patron, the standard "Web Search" option is your better choice.

Advanced Search

If you're still having trouble finding what you need, additional filtering is available via the Advanced Search page. Click on the gear icon in the upper right corner of your results page. From the pull-down menu, choose "Advanced Search." Figure 2.2 shows all the options available here.

To start with, you will have the usual word-limiting options.

The next section of the form is "Then narrow your results by . . ." Here you have more options that are specific to the type of search you are doing. For a web search, the options are:

- *Language*
  This field allows you to limit your results to only those in a particular language. At the time of this writing, there were more than 40 language choices, ranging from Afrikaans to Vietnamese. The default is "Any language."

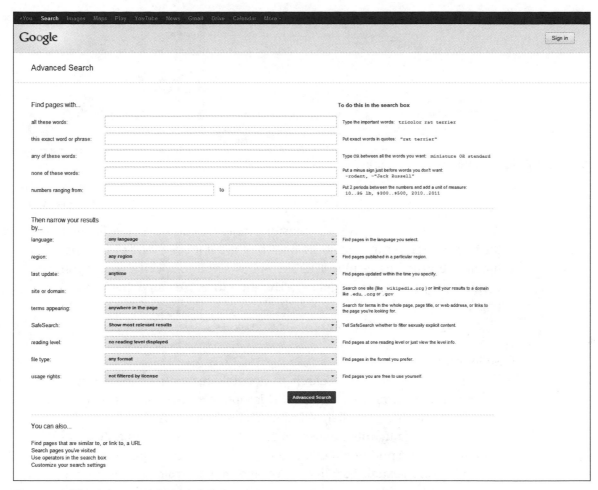

Figure 2.2 The Advanced Search interface

- *Region*

  Here you'll find a list of countries that Google can limit your results to, which is pretty much all of them, actually. Results in most cases will be from pages whose domain names contain the two-letter country code of the country you selected.

- *Last update*

  This field allows you to limit your results to pages that are from the Past 24 hours, Past week, Past month, or Past year. Please keep in mind that this date is based on the date of the page when last indexed, not the date on the live page as it is the moment you search.

- *Site or domain*

  This field allows you to limit your results to a particular domain or top level domain. For example, to retrieve results from only US government sites, enter *.gov*. To retrieve results from only Microsoft, enter *microsoft .com*.

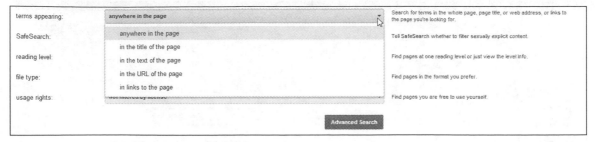

Figure 2.3 Advanced Search terms pull-down menu

- *Terms appearing*

  As mentioned earlier, Google considers many locations when looking for your search terms, including ones that are not even part of the documents returned as results. This field allows you to specify where you would like your terms to appear. These options are "anywhere in the page," "in the title of the page," "in the text of the page," "in the URL of the page," and "in links to the page" (figure 2.3).

- *SafeSearch*

  As we've mentioned, SafeSearch is Google's technology for filtering out potentially offensive content. This option allows you to change your browser settings to help eliminate adult content from your search results. By default, the SafeSearch filter is disabled. To enable Safe-Search, open the pull-down menu, then click on "Filter explicit results." This will filter sexually explicit video and images from Google Search result pages, as well as results that might link to explicit content. To disable the SafeSearch filter, open the menu again and click "Show most relevant results." Please be aware that no filter is perfect. Even Google says that "we do our best to keep SafeSearch as up-to-date and comprehensive as possible, but inappropriate sites will sometimes slip through the cracks."

- *Reading level*

  Limit your search results to a specific reading level: Basic, Intermediate, or Advanced, as shown in figure 2.4. You can also choose to see results annotated with reading levels, which includes a percentage breakdown of results by reading level.

- *File type*

  This field allows you to limit or exclude results in a particular file format, such as PDF, Postscript, Word, Excel, PowerPoint, and RTF (rich-text format). For example, many government reports are published in PDF format, so limiting to that format could make finding a particular report easier.

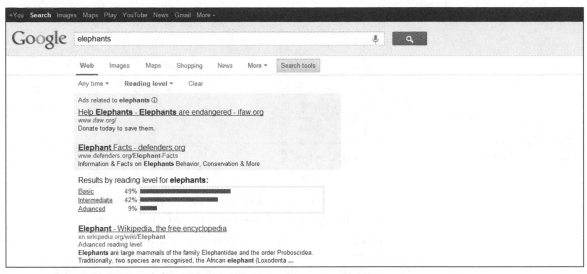

Figure 2.4 Advanced Search for *elephants,* reading level annotation

- *Usage rights*

  If you are planning to reuse someone else's content from the web, it's always a good idea to check the usage rights that the original owner may have placed on their pages. The Advanced Search usage rights filter can help you find content that you are allowed to use. The usage rights filter shows you pages that are either labeled with a Creative Commons license or labeled as being in the public domain.

  Creative Commons (http://creativecommons. org), a project started by Lawrence Lessig, allows content creators to assign a copyright-like license to their content, controlling attribution, commercial usage, and derivative creation. Once created, this license can be attached to the content, allowing users to know what permissions they do and do not have when it comes to using that content.

  But, before you use any content you find, you should check the actual license information on the original page. The Google Search usage rights filter can help you get started, but it should not be the only research you do before using someone else's content.

  The usage rights filtering options (figure 2.5) include:

  - Not filtered by license—limits your search results to pages on which Google could find no license or public domain indication.
  - Free to use or share—limits your search results to pages that are either labeled as public domain or carry a license that allows you to copy or redistribute its content, as long as the content remains unchanged.
  - Free to use, share, or modify—limits your search results to pages that are labeled with a license that allows you to copy, modify, or redistribute in ways specified in the license.

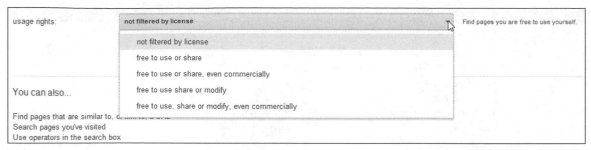

Figure 2.5 Advanced Search usage rights options

   - Commercially—Limits your search results to pages that are labeled with a license that allows you to use the content for commercial purposes, in ways specified in the license.

After setting any or all of these limiters, just click the "Advanced Search" button at the bottom right of the page to execute your search.

Web Search Results

When you do a general web search on Google, your search results will contain a little of everything. It will not be restricted to a certain type of result, as you will see in future chapters. Since you haven't yet chosen to focus on a particular type of result, Google will give you all of them.

There are some similarities across all search results pages, however. The search box, with your search terms included, is at the top, along with links related to your Google account and Google+ services. Just below this, the links to other types of searches are presented, followed by the Search tools link, which provides more search limiters. Next, you will find the number of results and the length of time it took Google to perform the search, and all the way to the right is the gear icon to access your general search settings, advanced search options, and web history. If there are any Ads or Sponsored links, they will appear at the top of your results and/or off to the right.

If you have done a search for a person, place, or thing, you will see a box to the right of your search results with information gathered via Google's Knowledge Graph. These are quick facts and/or pictures related to your search that have been gathered from various sources, such as Wikipedia, subject-specific resources such as Weather Underground for weather information and the World Bank for economic statistics, and publicly available data from Freebase. com, a free and open database of over 24 million things.

Depending on the topic of your search, you may also find a block of "In-depth articles" at the bottom of the first page of results. Google uses an algorithm to look for high-quality, in-depth content related to your search and presents them to you in case you want to learn more about the subject you are researching.

At the bottom of the page are the standard next/previous page of results links and some suggested searches related to your search term(s).

STANDARD RESULT

Your standard search results list will show the most relevant match first, followed by the next relevant match, and so on (figure 2.6). A typical result will include:

- Title of the web page: This is a hot link that you can click to go to the web page.
- URL: In green, you'll see the web address of that result's web page.
- Snippet: A few lines of text excerpted from the web page.

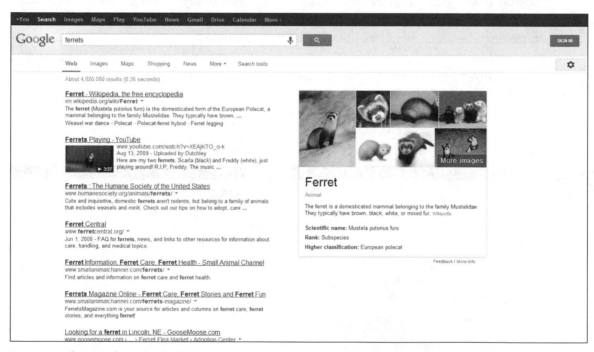

Figure 2.6 Google Search results for *ferrets*

At the end of the URL, you will see a green down arrow. Click it to get a drop-down menu with up to three options. The first option is Cached, which will bring up the cached view of the page, a snapshot of the page as it appeared at a particular time. The second option is Similar, which will bring up a list of pages like that page. If you are logged in to your Google account, it will also show a Share option, so that you can share the result on Google+.

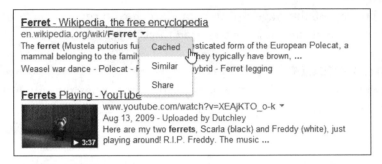

Figure 2.7 Google Search results drop-down menu

You can add more terms to your basic search to make it return the type of search result you want. For example, if what you really wanted was to see pictures of ferrets, add the word *pictures* to your *ferrets* search. We can see the difference between searches in the following examples.

- How to get Image results (figure 2.8)
- How to get Video results (figure 2.9)
- How to get News results (figure 2.10)

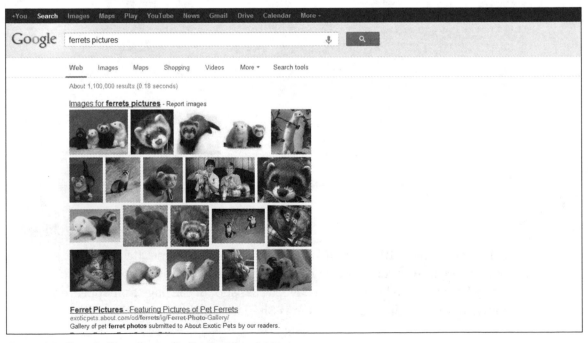

Figure 2.8 Google Search results for *ferrets pictures*

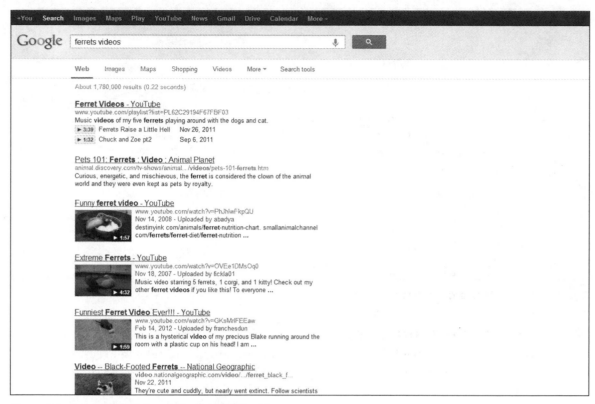

Figure 2.9 Google Search results for *ferrets videos*

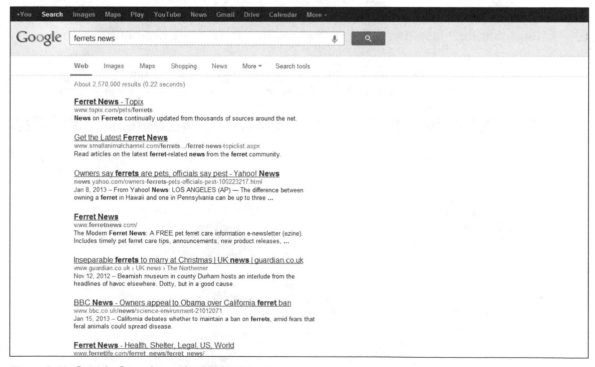

Figure 2.10 Google Search results for *ferrets news*

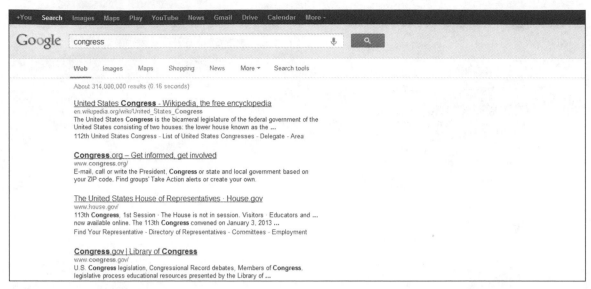

Figure 2.11 Google Search results for *congress*

LINKS WITHIN SNIPPETS

For some results, Google provides links within the snippet to relevant sections of the page, making it faster and easier to find what you're looking for (figure 2.11).

RESULTS WITH SITE LINKS AND SEARCH WITHIN THE SITE

If Google thinks it will be useful to a user, site links are showcased in a search result (figure 2.12). An automated algorithm analyzes websites, looking for links that may help users jump quickly to the section they need of the main website.

In addition, if other algorithms determine that more refined searching within a site may be useful, there is a search box below the site links. This

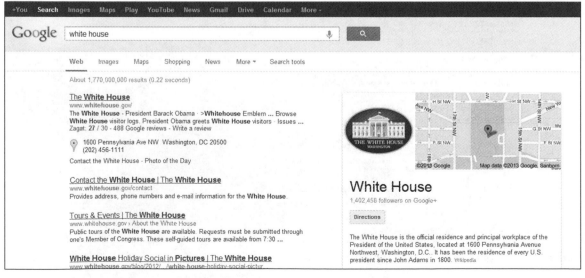

Figure 2.12 Google Search results for *white house*

search box gives you the ability to search only within that site for information you need.

Search Results Options and Tools

You can further refine your search using the filtering options in the panel above your search results. The options available will vary depending on your original search, so you won't always see all the possible limiters.

If you would like to limit your search to certain types of content, you can switch to see results such as Images or Videos. Click "More" to see all the options. To see all types of content, choose "Web."

Click "Search tools" for even more ways to limit your results (figure 2.13). Three pull-down menus will appear below the content options: Time, Results and Location.

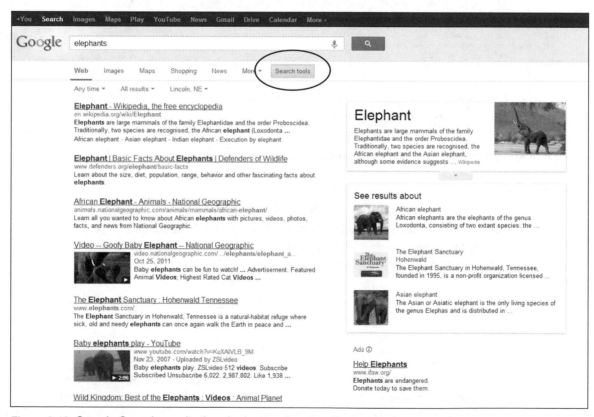

Figure 2.13 Google Search results for *elephants,* showing filtering options.

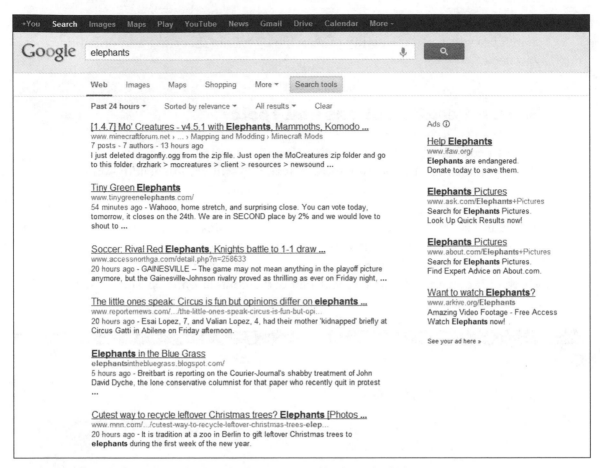

Figure 2.14 Google Search results for *elephants*, posted in the past 24 hours

- *Time*
  This option limits your results to items posted during the following times: Past hour, Past 24 hours, Past week, Past month, Past year; or with "Custom range . . ." you can enter specific dates (figure 2.14). Click on "Any time" to return to the full results list.

The second Search tools menu is Results. By default it is set to All Results. Other limiters that might be available are:

- *Sites with images*
  This limits your search results to pages with images on them, and shows a selection of those images, to help you decide if the entire site is what you're looking for (figure 2.15).

- *Related searches*
  This gives you suggestions for other terms to combine with your original search term(s) that might help you narrow your search further. It will also show other terms that may be similar to your original search term(s) (figure 2.16).

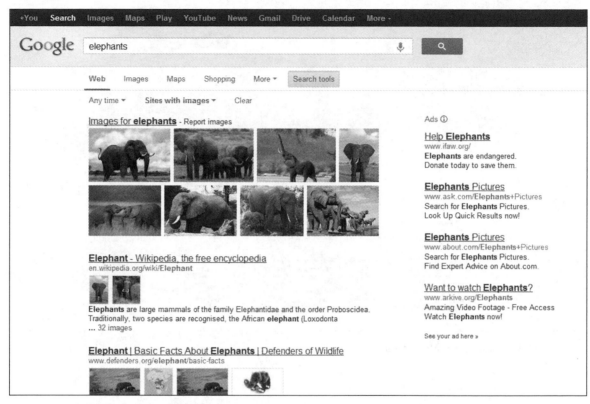

Figure 2.15 Sites with images: *elephants*

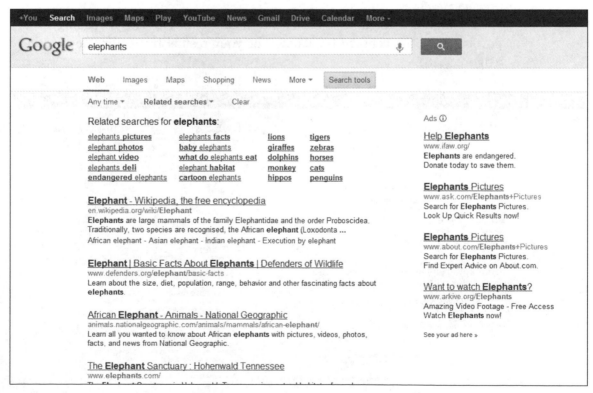

Figure 2.16 Related searches for *elephants*

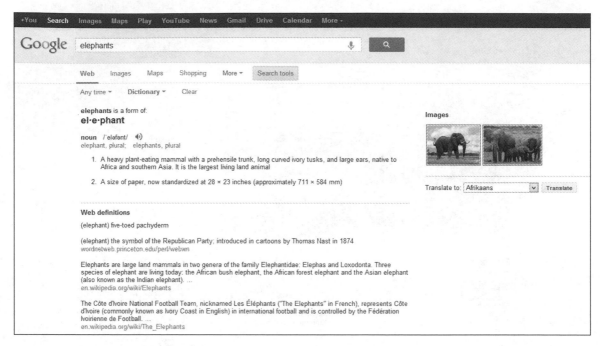

Figure 2.17 Definitions for *elephants*

- *Dictionary*
  This option brings up a definition of your search term (figure 2.17).

- *Reading level*
  See results annotated with Basic, Intermediate, or Advanced reading levels, and a percentage breakdown of your results by reading level (figure 2.18).

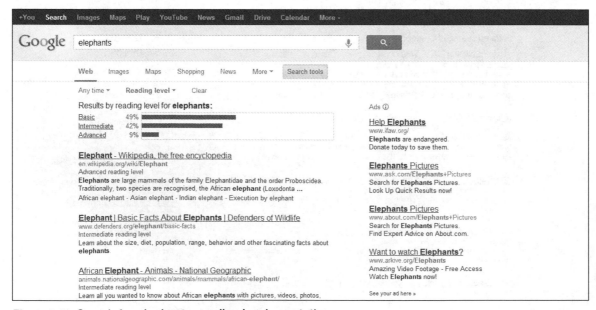

Figure 2.18 Search for *elephants*, reading level annotation

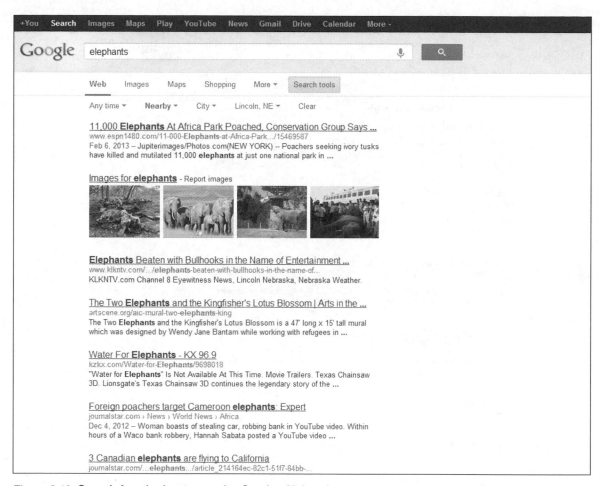

Figure 2.19 Search for *elephants*, nearby Omaha, Nebraska

- *Nearby*

  This works geographically, using your IP address or your default location, to limit your search results to items that are relevant to that location (figure 2.19). You can narrow down your results to the city, region, or state level.

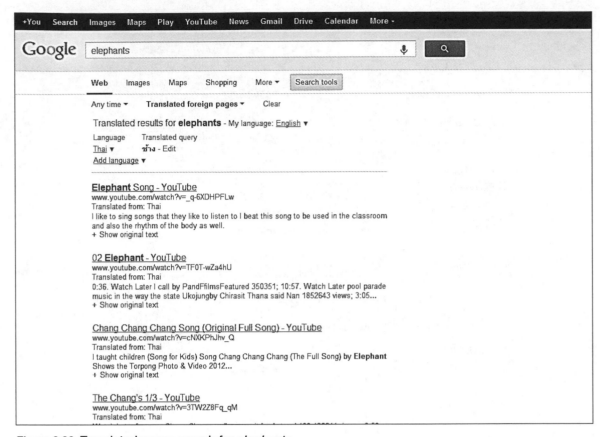

Figure 2.20 Translated pages search for *elephants*

- *Translated foreign pages*

  This option uses Google's automatic translator service, Google Translate. Google translates your search term into one or more languages and then performs a search using the translated terms. The search results are then translated back into your default language (figure 2.20). Click a translated result and you'll be taken to an automatically translated version of the page.

- *Verbatim*

  Google typically tries to help you get to the information you need by automatically improving the searches you enter. Some of the improvements Google makes are suggesting spelling corrections and alternative spellings, including synonyms of your search terms to find related results, and searching for words with the same stem, such as *running* when you search for *run*. To see results that contain the exact words you are searching for, click "Verbatim," and Google will ignore these usual improvements and search only for the exact words you entered.

Figure 2.21 Location menu for *elephants*

The third Search tools option is Location. The location used to customize your results is shown. Google's location detection technology automatically sets a location for you using your IP address, but you can change that location to anyplace you like and then save it as your default location.

chapter 3

Google Images

WITH OVER 10 billion images indexed, and more added every day as the web grows, Google Images is a vast resource of photos and graphics. Google automatically searches the web, looking for images on all sorts of websites, such as bloggers, media outlets, and stock photo sites, and then indexes them using captions, descriptions, and other information found within the images.

Basic Searching

There are multiple ways to search for images via Google. First there is the Google Images search page at http://images.google.com/ (figure 3.1). You can also do a web search on the Google home page and then limit your results to the images media type. Lastly, as described in chapter 2, images may appear as results to a web search.

Figure 3.1 Google Images search screen

Enter your search terms to find images relevant to your need or interest, then click the "Search" icon (figure 3.2).

Above your image results, Google will suggest Related Searches that might help you narrow down your search more. Hover your cursor over the suggested searches to see a few sample images. When you click on a single image, it will enlarge that image in an inline panel just below that row of images and

Figure 3.2 Google Images search results for *lincoln memorial*

give you more information about it—the file name for the image, the URL where the original image can be found, its size in pixels, and a link to retrieve More sizes of this image (figure 3.3). There are also buttons to Visit the page that this image is located on, View the original image alone, and to get Image details. The "Image details" button is actually doing a Search by Image, which is detailed later in this chapter.

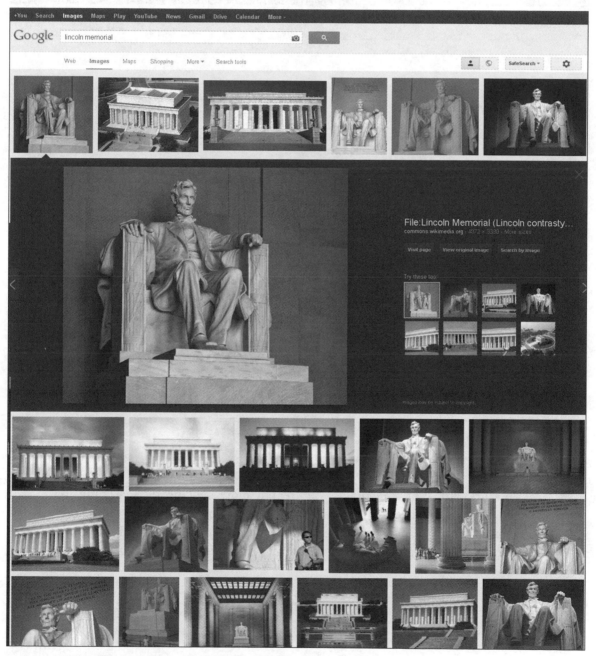

Figure 3.3 Selecting an image from the search results

Advanced Image Search

If you're still having trouble finding what you need, additional filtering is available via the Advanced Image Search page. Click on the gear icon in the upper right corner of your Image results page. From the pull-down menu, choose "Advanced Search" (figure 3.4).

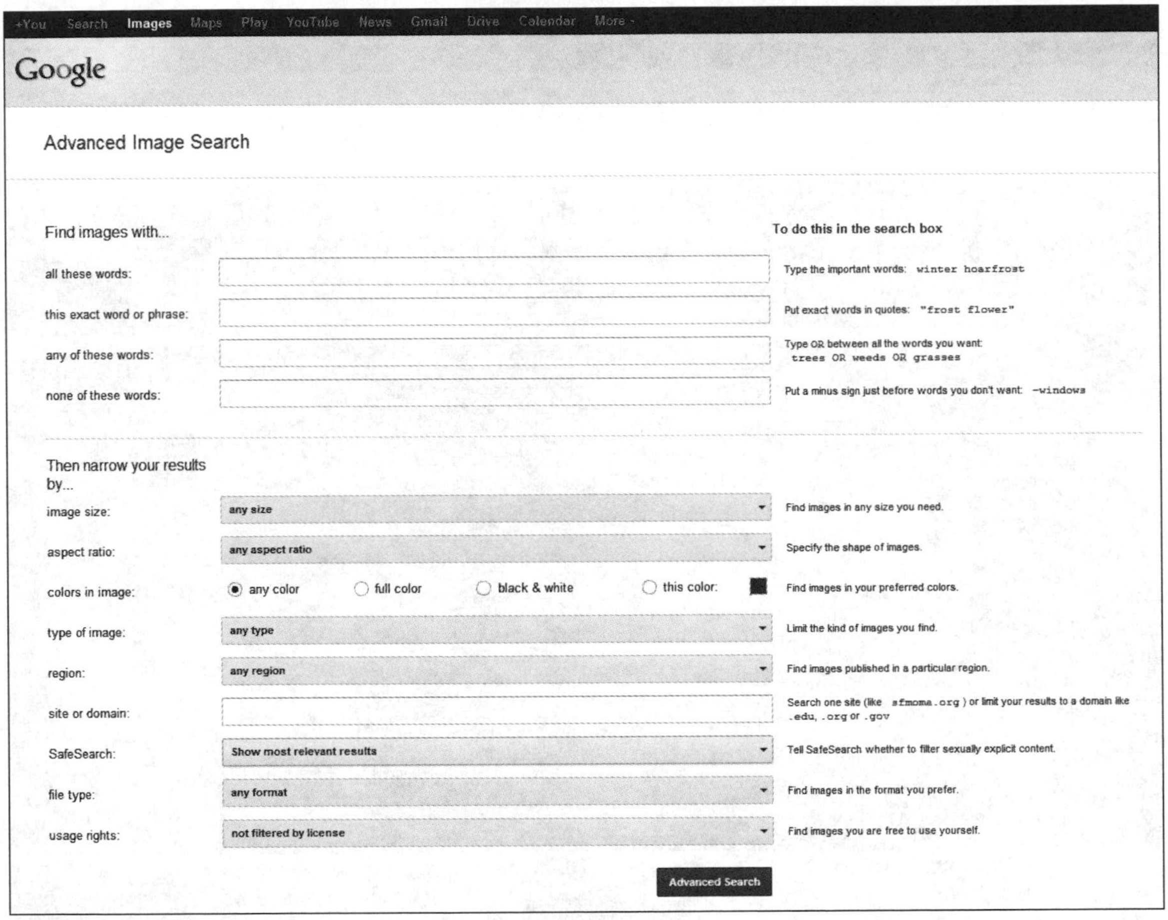

Figure 3.4 Advanced Search pull-down menu

To start with, you can make your search more specific by searching for an exact word or phrase by putting it in quotes. You can make your search broader by using OR between terms to expand the results. You can also exclude certain terms by using a minus sign in front of the word you don't want to use (figure 3.5).

The Advanced Image Search page offers additional image related limits:

- *Image size*
  Choose the size of the image that you need: Any size, Large, Medium, Icon, or Larger than a certain size.

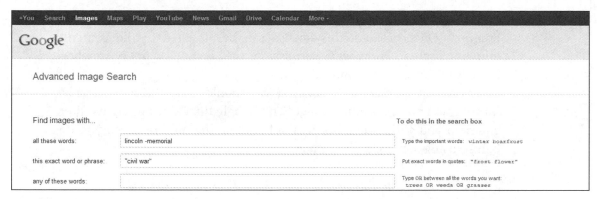

Figure 3.5 Advanced Image Search word limiting

- *Aspect ratio*
  Choose the shape of the image: Tall, Square, Wide, or Panoramic.

- *Colors in image*
  Choose your preferred colors: any color, full color, or black-and-white, or choose from the color blocks.

- *Type of image*
  Choose the kind of image you need: face, photo, clip art, or line drawing.

- *Region*
  Search for images geographically, using the pull-down menu to choose a country.

- *Site or domain*
  Enter a particular URL to search, or a particular domain, such as .gov or .org.

- *File type*
  Limit your results to images of a particular format: JPG, GIF, PNG, BMP, SVG, WEBP, or ICO.

- *Usage rights*
  Again, if you are planning to reuse someone else's content from the web, it's always a good idea to check the usage rights that the original owner may have placed on their image. The Advanced Image Search usage rights filter can help you find images that you are allowed to use. The usage rights filter shows you pages that are either labeled with a Creative Commons license or labeled as being in the public domain. Creative Commons (http://creativecommons. org), a project started by Lawrence Lessig, allows content creators to assign a copyright-like license to their content, controlling attribution, commercial usage, and derivative

creation. Once created, this license can be attached to the content, allowing users to know what permissions they do and do not have when it comes to using that content.

Before you use any image you find, you should check the actual license information on the original image. The Google Images usage rights filter can help you get started, but it should not be the only research you do before using someone else's image.

The usage rights filtering options (figure 3.6) include:

- Not filtered by license—limits your search to images for which Google could find no license or public domain indication.
- Free to use or share—limits your search results to images that are either labeled as public domain or carry a license that allows you to copy or redistribute its content, as long as the content remains unchanged.
- Free to use, share, or modify—limits your search results to images that are labeled with a license that allows you to copy, modify, or redistribute in ways specified in the license.
- Commercially—limits your search results to images that are labeled with a license that allows you to use the image for commercial purposes, in ways specified in the license.

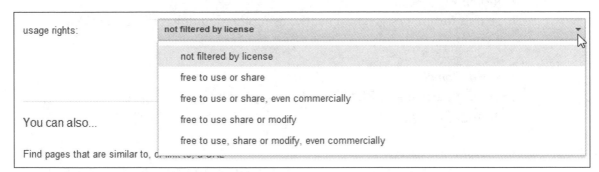

Figure 3.6 Advanced Image Search usage rights options

Search by Image

Rather than searching for an image, you can also search using an image as your search "term," so to speak. Using computer vision techniques, Google matches your image to other images on the web. Then, they attempt to generate a "best guess" text description of your image, and they also look for other images that have the same content as your original search image. Your results will include not only related images, but also websites relevant to your search image.

There are four ways you can Search by Image.

1. *Enter an image URL.*

You've found an image on the web, and you'd like to find other similar images or information about the image. Right-click on the image and select the option to Copy it. Then, go to http://images.google.com/ and click on the camera icon at the end of the search box. In the pop-out window that appears, paste in the URL you copied and click the "Search" button (figure 3.7).

Figure 3.7 Search by Image search screen, copied URL

2. *Upload an image.*

Say you have an image on your computer that you'd like to use to run your search. Go to http://images.google.com/ and click on the camera icon at the end of the search box. In the pop-out window that appears, click "Upload an Image," then Browse on your computer until you find the image you need. Select the image and Google will upload the image from your computer and run a search based on it. If Google can't generate a text description of your image, it will suggest that you enter some words in the search box. Then it runs a search using a combination of the image you uploaded and the words you entered (figure 3.8).

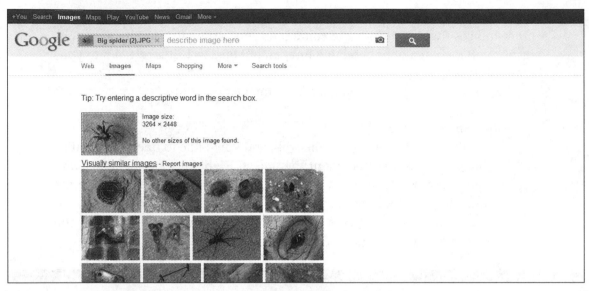

Figure 3.8 Search by Image search results of uploading file "big spider (2)"

3. Drag and drop an image.

Perhaps you've done an Image search and have found a new picture you'd like to base your search on. You can Click and Drag the image into the Google Images search box. Click on the image, hold down the mouse button, and drag it toward the Search box (figure 3.9). It will let you know when you can let go of the mouse button and drop the image into the Search box.

4. Use Firefox or Chrome browser extensions.

If you use Chrome or Firefox, Google offers browser extensions. After you have downloaded the extension you want, you can right click on

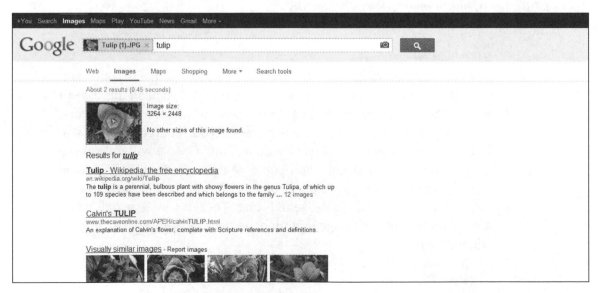

Figure 3.9 Search by Image dragging "Tulip (1)" image file into search box and adding the search term *tulip*

any image you find on the web and run a search based on that image. See Firefox extension: https://addons.mozilla.org/en-US/firefox/addon/ search-by-image-by-google/ (figure 3.10) and Chrome extension: https://chrome.google.com/webstore/detail/dajedkncpodkggklbeg ccjpmnglmnflm?hl = en (figure 3.11).

Figure 3.10 Search by Image Firefox extension

Figure 3.11 Search by Image Chrome extension

Search by Image Results Page

The results page for a Search by Image will look different from the usual Image results. Elements that you might see, depending on what Google was able to find, are shown in figure 3.12:

- *Preview image*
  A small version of the image that you searched with appears at the top of the results. That image is also in front of the search box, so you can combine other terms with the image, if needed.

Figure 3.12 Search by Image results page for a photo of cute dogs

- *Best guess*
Google offers its best guess at a text description for your image, which is also a link that you can then use to run a further search. Included with it are a couple of results using that best-guess text.

- *Visually similar images*
A set of images that Google has determined look similar to your original search image are presented. It also offers a link to see additional images that are similar.

- *Pages that include matching images*
If Google has found your exact image, the results will include the web pages that have your image on their site.

- *Other searches related to this image*
If Google isn't sure about its best-guess text description, it gives you its other guesses from which you can select to run a new search.

SafeSearch

Working in libraries, and with the public, you will often want or need to prevent objectionable adult images from appearing in your search results. SafeSearch allows you to change your browser settings to block this material. As you know, no filter is perfect, but SafeSearch does a pretty good job of filtering out most objectionable content. To identify this content, Google uses automated algorithms that look at many factors, including keywords, links, and images.

After you run your image search, there will be a SafeSearch pull-down menu above your search results (figure 3.13). By default, the SafeSearch fil-

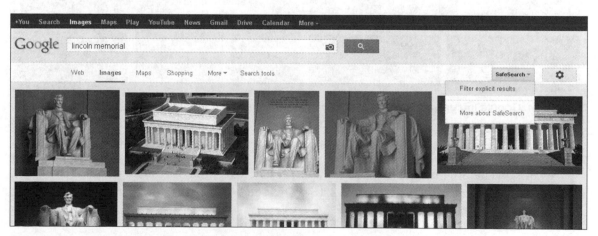

Figure 3.13 Google Images search results SafeSearch pull-down menu

ter is disabled. To enable SafeSearch, open the pull-down menu, then click on "Filter explicit results." This will filter sexually explicit video and images from Google Search result pages, as well as results that might link to explicit content. To disable the SafeSearch filter, open the menu again and click "Filter explicit results" to uncheck the option.

The Images Search results options and tools

You can further refine your search using the filtering options in the panel above your search results. If you would like to expand your search to other types of content besides Images, you can switch to see results such as Videos or News. To see all types of content, choose "Web."

Click "Search tools" for the image-specific filters. The following pull-down menus will appear below the content options:

- *Date*
  Limit your results to images from the Past 24 hours, Past week, or a Custom range. How many days ago the image was added will be indicated on each image (figure 3.14).

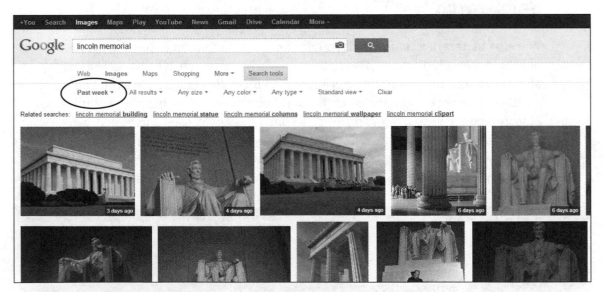

Figure 3.14 Google Images search results for *lincoln memorial,* past week

- *Sort by Subject*
  The Sort by Subject option will present your image results sorted into subject categories (figure 3.15). Click on "All Results" to go back to the unsorted images.

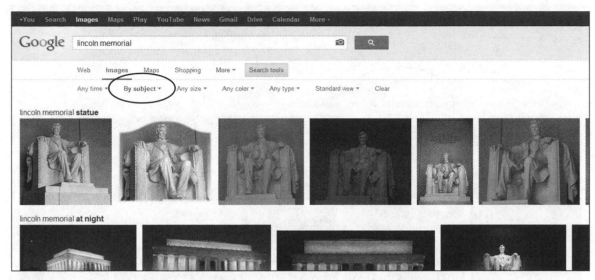

Figure 3.15 Google Images search results for *lincoln memorial* sorted by subject

- *Size*
  Use the Size options to show images of a certain size.

  Large—images with resolutions bigger than 1024 x 768 pixels.
  Medium—images with resolutions between 400 x 300 pixels and
  1024 x 768 pixels.
  Icon—square images with the following resolutions: 50 x 50, 64 x
  64, 96 x 96, 128 x 128, and 256 x 256 (figure 3.16).
  Larger than . . . —choose the minimum size you want from the pull-
  down menu (figure 3.17).
  Exactly . . . —enter the width and height you're looking for, then
  click "Search" (figure 3.18).

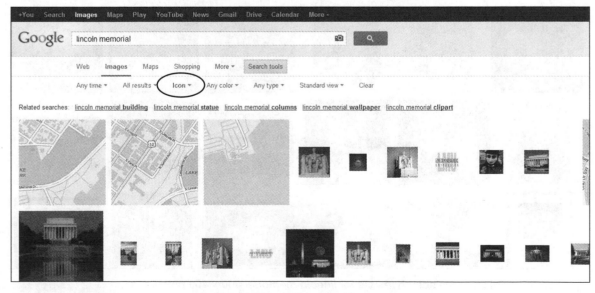

Figure 3.16 Google Images search results for *lincoln memorial,* icon sizes

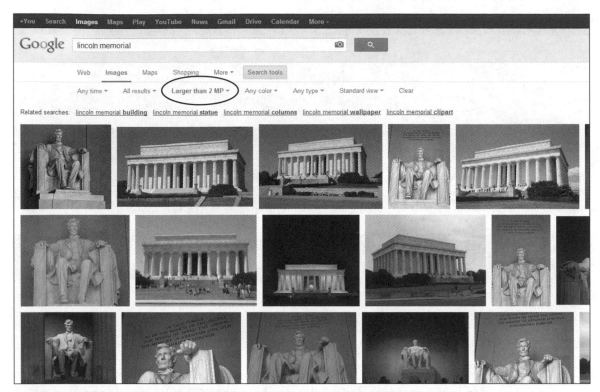

Figure 3.17 Google Images search results for *lincoln memorial* choosing minimum size

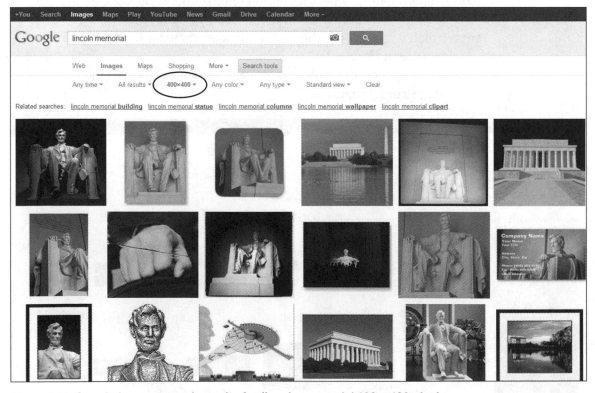

Figure 3.18 Google Images search results for *lincoln memorial* 400 x 400 pixels

- *Color*

  You can choose full-color or black-and-white images. Using the color blocks, you can find images that predominantly contain that color, as shown in the following examples (figures 3.19, 3.20, 3.21).

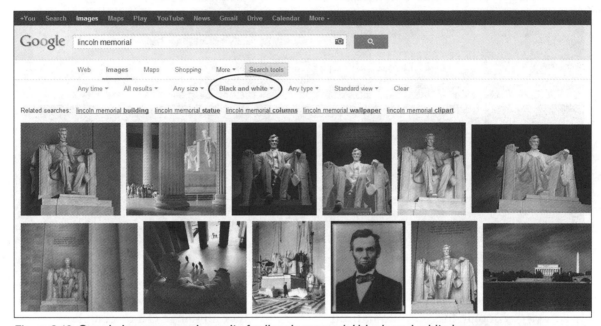

Figure 3.19 Google Images search results for *lincoln memorial* black-and-white images

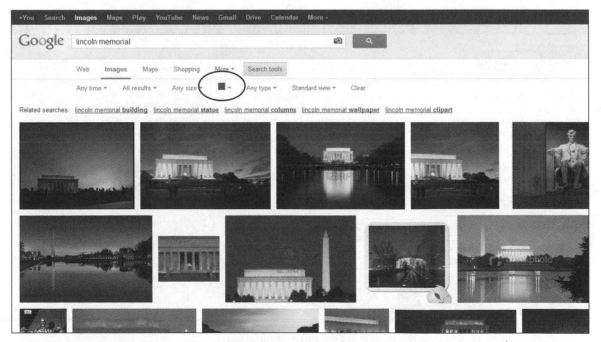

Figure 3.20 Google Images search results for *lincoln memorial*, color purple

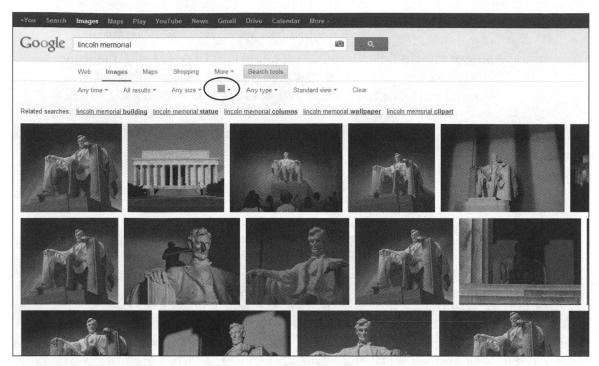

Figure 3.21 Google Images search results for *lincoln memorial*, color orange

- *Type*

  Google Images automatically detects whether an image is a face, a photograph, clip art, or a line drawing (figure 3.22). Clicking "Any type" will return you to your unfiltered results.

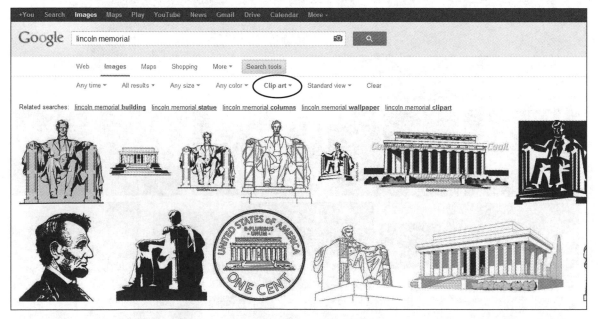

Figure 3.22 Google Images search results for *lincoln memorial* clip art

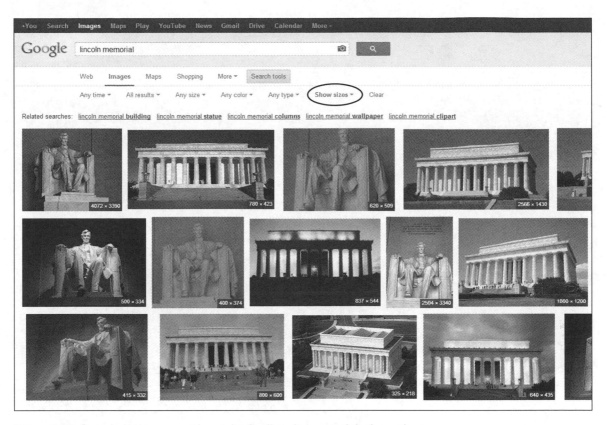

Figure 3.23 Google Images search results for *lincoln memorial*, show sizes

- *View*
  Clicking "Show sizes" will display the image sizes of the results (figure 3.23).

Conclusion

When Google first started indexing the web, pictures and images were not as prevalent as they are today. Over the years, as the web has grown and changed, the methods to search for what we want have required changing as well. Google Images has evolved into a very useful resource for people looking for anything picture-related. Both librarians and patrons can use the features that Google has developed to find the images they need.

chapter 4

Google News

AS YOU QUICKLY notice when you reach the Google News home page (http://
news.google.com), Google News is more than just a search engine for news-
based content. It is also a portal to news content from all over the web. Since
the focus of this book is searching Google, this chapter focuses mostly on just
that. However, to ignore the layout and content of the Google News home page
we feel would be a disservice to the reader. So, before we get into the searching
features of Google News, let's take a brief tour of the Google News home page.

The News Home Page

As we've already mentioned, the Google News home page is very different
from most of the other search home pages (figure 4.1). It's almost as if Google

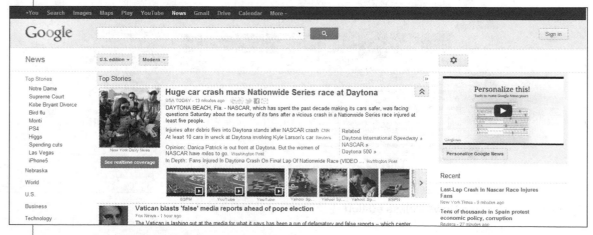

Figure 4.1 The Google News home page

News is living a double life. The first is as a news portal, giving you access to headlines from various sources on various topics. The second is as a search engine through which you can find news about the topic of your choosing.

In this section we take a look at the portal end of things, everything below the search box. Once we get through that, we focus the majority of this chapter on the search-engine end.

By default, the Google News home page is presented in three columns. On the left is a list of links giving you access to top stories in various categories along with links for current top stories. In the middle column are the stories themselves. Selecting a link in the left column will change the content in the middle. The column on the right contains links to additional stories in categories such as Recent, News near you, and Editor's picks. Clicking any of these links will open a new window or tab containing the source web page for that story.

EDITIONS AND LAYOUT

There are two gray buttons near the top center of the page labeled (in our example) "US edition" and "Modern." The first button controls which "edition" or content Google News is currently showing you. Clicking this button will provide you with a list of more than 50 countries and/or languages to choose from. For example, choosing "Pokska" will change the content to Poland-related news stories in Polish, as shown in figure 4.2.

Clicking on the "Modern" button will control the layout of the page. Your choices are Modern (default), Headlines, Compact, and Classic, as shown in figures 4.3 through 4.6.

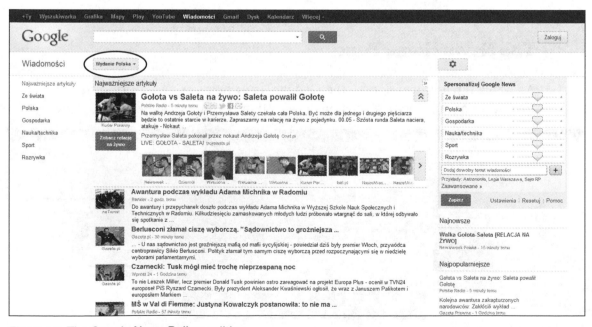

Figure 4.2 The Google News Polksa edition

As you can see, the layout options control the presentation of news stories in the central column of the page

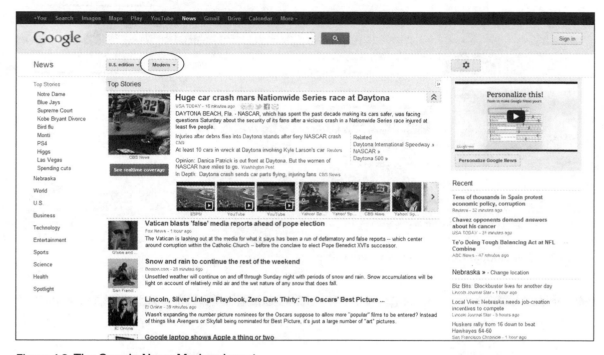

Figure 4.3 The Google News Modern layout

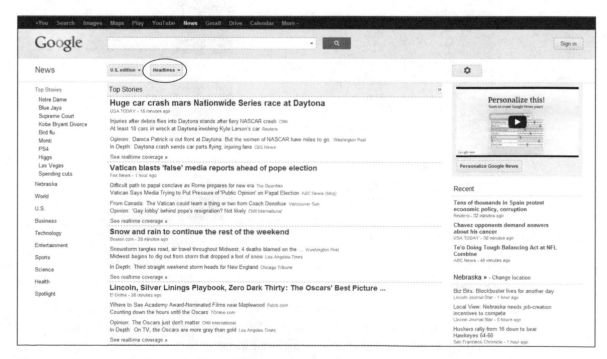

Figure 4.4 The Google News Headlines layout

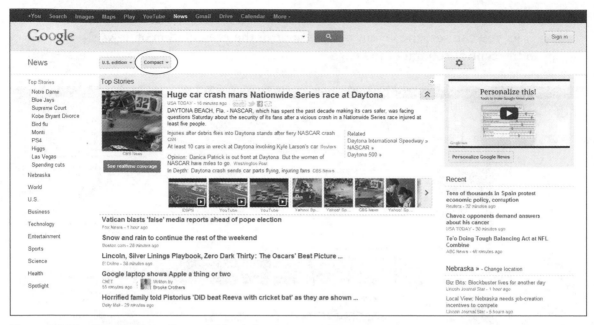

Figure 4.5 The Google News Compact layout

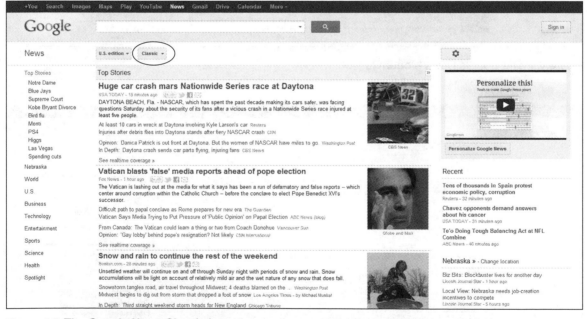

Figure 4.6 The Google News Classic layout

TOP STORIES

The center column starts with the current top stories for your selected edition. We stay with the US edition for our example. Other than changing the edition being displayed, there are also three additional buttons (highlighted in figure 4.7) that you should be aware of.

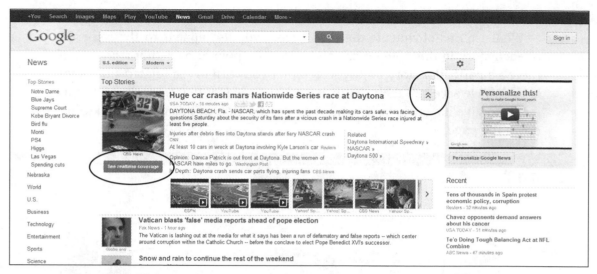

Figure 4.7 Top Stories tool buttons

The first is a » located to the right of Top Stories. Clicking this icon will hide the right column and expand the width of the center column all the way to the right side of your browser's window. The ˄ icon, located to the right of the headline of the top story, will toggle between showing and hiding the related articles for the current top story.

The third button is to the left of the current top story and is labeled "See realtime coverage." Clicking this button will take you to a new page showing real-time coverage of that story, including live-updated headlines, Google+ discussions, and an article timeline (figure 4.8). If you're looking for up-to-the-minute coverage of a breaking story, this is the page you want to be on.

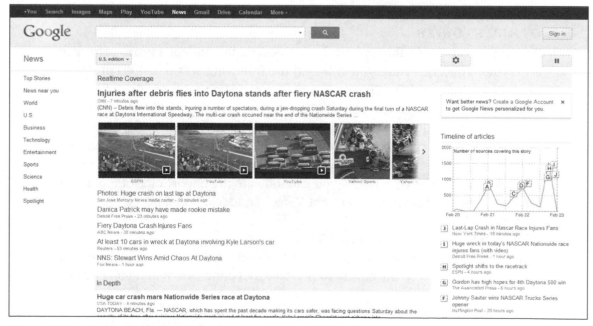

Figure 4.8 Realtime coverage of "Huge car crash mars Nationwide Series race at Daytona"

What isn't as obvious is that the ⌃ icon will also appear to the top-right of each story in this column as you hover your pointer over that story. So, if there's a particular story on the screen that you wish to see related stories for and/or have access to their realtime coverage page for that story, just find this icon and give it a click. Figure 4.9 shows an example of this for a story farther down the page.

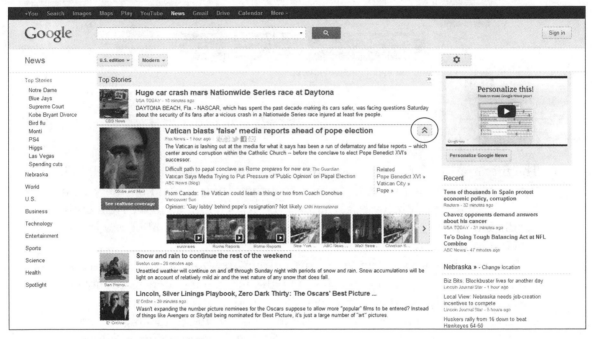

Figure 4.9 Expanding a story to see related stories

OTHER STORIES

The right column of this page contains additional content that is refreshed each time you visit. Here you will find the following sections: Recent, News near you (along with a "Change location" link if you wish to see news from another location or Google just thinks you're somewhere you're not), Google News Badges (an attempt to turn news reading into a game, similar to badges you can earn for checking in to different types of places with Foursquare), Editor's Picks (which contains buttons to move from one content source to another and a slider with which you can indicate the importance of a particular news source), Spotlight, Spotlight Video, and Most Popular.

NEWS HOME PAGE SETTINGS

Lastly, we want to take a brief look at the gear icon at the top right of the page, which gives you the ability to personalize your news. When you click on

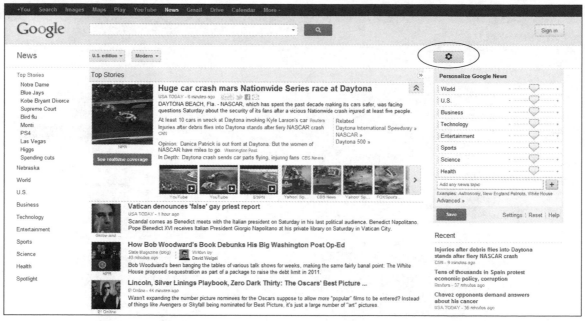

Figure 4.10 Personalize Google News settings

this icon, a new section will appear in the right column that gives you several options for customizing this page (figure 4.10).

- *Category sliders*
  Here you can choose how important different categories of news are. Each slider has stops for (from left to right,) Rarely, Occasionally, Sometimes, Often, and Always. The less important (slide to the left) a category is, the less likely a story in that category will appear on the home page. Conversely, the more important you consider a category (slide to the right), the more likely stories from the category will appear.

  Here you can also rearrange the categories through drag-and-drop, and remove a category by hovering over it and clicking the trash can icon.

- *Add any news topic*
  If the above list doesn't have a category listed that you want to include, you can add that here. For example, if you're a fan of author Dean Koontz, you could add his name here and then move the slider to the important end of the scale.

- *Advanced*
  Clicking on the "Advanced" link will take you to the Custom Sections Directory Page, which gives you many more options and suggestions for

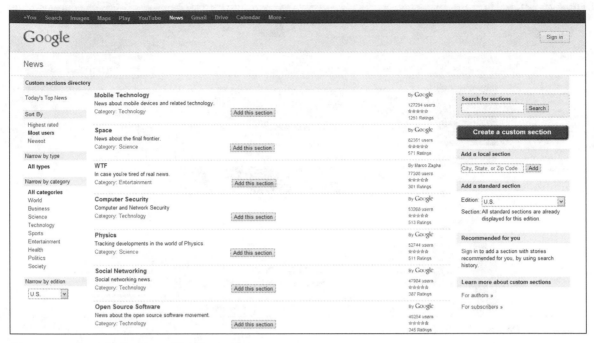

Figure 4.11 Custom Sections Directory page

manipulating the categories of news items to be shown on the Google News home page. Please refer to figure 4.11 to see an example of the options that are available here.

- *Adjust sources*
  Similarly to the adjustment and addition or subtraction of categories, you can also add, remove, and determine the importance of news sources. In our example, you can see that because we live in Nebraska we've added the *Lincoln Journal Star* as an important source while setting the *New York Daily News* to be used as a source Rarely.

There are also three links at the bottom of this area: Settings, Reset, and Help. Clicking the "Settings" link will take you to the Google News Settings page and provide you with the following options:

- *Sources*
  This section allows you to "Personalize Google News to reflect your taste in publishers." Here you can choose to set how many Blogs and Press Releases to be included: None, Fewer, Normal, or More.

- *News home page*
  Here you can set the home page to "View as:" in a single column or two columns. This ignores the column on the left, which displays story categories. Here you also have the options to "Open articles in a new

browser window" or not, "Automatically reload the page every fifteen minutes" or not, "Show Google News Badges" or not, and "Show Google+ posts in main column" or not.

If you've made any changes, be sure to click the "Save changes" button before navigating away from this page.

Finally, the "Reset" link will undo any changes you've made to these settings, and the "Help" link gives further assistance. And as usual, don't forget to click the blue "Save" button to keep your changes.

Now that we've got all that covered, let's dive in to searching Google News.

Basic Search

There isn't much to say about the Google News basic search that you haven't read already in this book. Enter your keywords here and press enter or click the blue search icon to initiate your search. The search performed by default will be a "with all words" search and you will be presented with a search results page, which we describe later in this chapter.

However, there is one little trick available here that is shown in figure 4.12. As we've already mentioned, pressing the enter key will initiate a news search. However, pressing Shift-Enter will initiate a Google Web Search instead. This can come in handy if you're already on a page of news results and would like a quick keyboard shortcut to a web search.

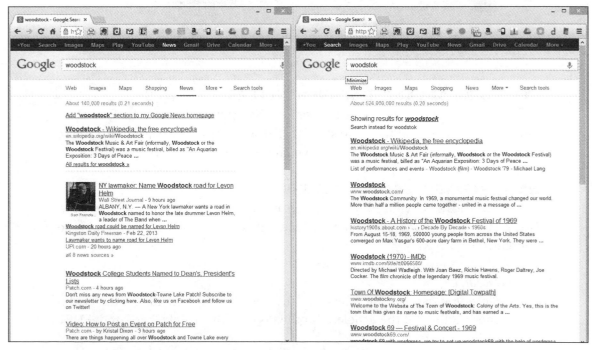

Figure 4.12 The difference between Enter and Shift-Enter in the Google News search

Advanced Search

As with a few other Google search interfaces, the News advanced search is no longer presented on a separate page. Instead it is integrated into the basic search field and can be found by clicking the down-pointing triangle at the far right of the search box. Clicking this icon will bring up the advanced search options immediately below the search box. (See figure 4.13.)

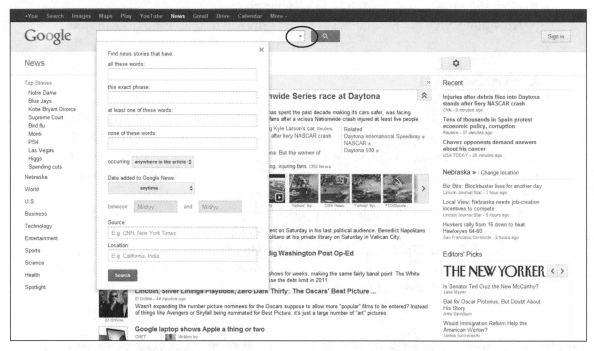

Figure 4.13 The Google News advanced search interface

STANDARD ADVANCED SEARCH FILTERS
As with all Google searches, the Advanced News search offers the four standard search filters: "all these words," "this exact phrase," "at least one of these words," and "none of these words," which we covered in chapter 2.

NEWS SPECIFIC SEARCH FILTERS
When it comes to advanced search filters in Google News, there are only four. However, they are important options when it comes to searching news-based content.

- *Occurring*
  Here you can choose between "anywhere in the article" (default), "in the headline of the article," "in the body of the article," or "in the URL of the article."

- *Date added to Google News*

  When searching for news, the time frame in which the story was published can be crucial. Here you can choose from "anytime" (default), "last hour," "last day," "past week," "past month," "specified dates," or "in archive."

  If you choose "specified dates," the fields for "between [date] and [date]" will become available for you to enter a starting and/or ending date. In this case the date should be entered in month/day/year format. (In non-US editions, your dates may need to be entered in day/month/year format. Refer to the in-field prompts as needed.)

  Choosing "in archive" performs your search in Google's News Archive, which includes "both partner content digitized by Google through our News Archives Partner Program and online archival materials that we've crawled." You can learn more about the content of the News Archive at http://support.google.com/news/bin/answer.py?hl=en&answer=1638638

- *Source*

  Here you can enter one or more sources that you wish to limit your search to. If you enter more than one source, do so as a comma delimited list. For example: *Lincoln Journal Star, Omaha World Herald.*

- *Location*

  If you wish to limit your results to stories from a particular location, you may enter it here. Location can be as broad as a country or as specific as a city and state.

Results

Once you've performed your search, you'll be presented with your results page (figure 4.14). However, unique to Google News results, the first item listed is not a search result but instead a link labeled "Add "[search terms]" to Google News Homepage." Clicking this link will add your current search terms as a topic, as discussed earlier under Personalize Google News. Once it's been added there, you can return to the personalization options and edit its level of inclusion.

After the "Add" link you will see your actual search results. Each result includes the following information, if available:

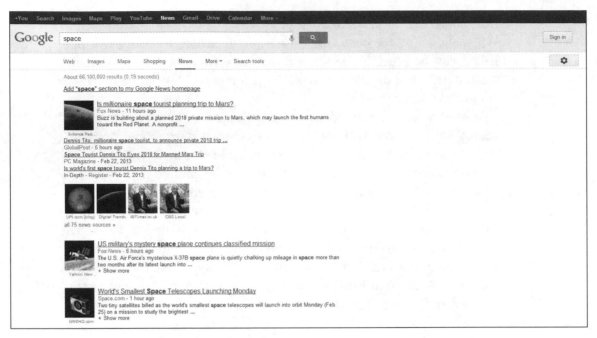

Figure 4.14 Sample Google News search results

- *Title*

  The title of the article, which is hyperlinked to the full article online

- *Source*

  The name of the publication or domain name of the website where the story has been published

- *Age*

  Either the date the story was originally published (usually for print publications), such as "Jun 17, 2012," or how long ago the story way published (usually for online-only publications such as blogs), such as "11 hours ago" or "6 days ago"

- *Snippet*

  A short bit of content from the story, usually about two lines, which contains your search terms in bold

- *Similar articles*

  If appropriate, Google will provide a short list of articles that are similar in content to a story provided as a search result. If there are more than a few, an additional link will be provided to see all the related stories.

- *Photo*

  If a relevant photo is available from the source article, a thumbnail version of that image will appear to the right of the search result, along with a caption giving the source of the image. Clicking on the image will also take you to the source web page for the result.

At the bottom of the search results page you'll also be given a link to "Create an email alert for [search terms]." Clicking this link will take you to the "Create an Alert" page in Google Alerts. We cover the details of this feature in chapter 11.

GOOGLE NEWS SEARCH RESULTS OPTIONS AND TOOLS

The content search limiters in this panel can be found in the Google Web Search (and most other searches) and have been described in detail in chapter 2.

The Google News Search tools contain three options. The first pull-down menu gives you the choice between "All news" or just "Blogs."

The other two menus are:

- *Date*

  Any time, Past hour, Past 24 hours, Past week, Past month, Archives, Custom range . . .

- *Sort*

  Sorted by relevance, Sorted by date

chapter 5

Google Videos

YOU MAY BE thinking, "Why is there a chapter on Google Video in this book? Didn't Google shut down their video sharing service and purchase YouTube?" And you would be correct. Yes, they did. In 2009 Google stopped accepting uploads to Google Video. Google bought YouTube in 2006, and in 2011, they started migrating Google Video files into YouTube. This migration was completed in summer 2012.

When Google retired Google Video, they switched their focus to search technology. Now the service is called Google Videos (plural) and indexes millions of videos from all over the Internet. You can search for and watch an ever-growing collection of TV shows, movie clips, music videos, documentaries, personal productions, and more. And Google has created many ways for you to search to find just the video you need.

Basic Searching

There are several ways you can search for videos with Google. You can start your search at the Google Videos website, http://videos.google.com, which is what this chapter will be focusing on (figure 5.1). You can also do a web search and then select the video content type, as we showed in chapter 1. When you do a web search, videos may be included in those search results. Lastly you can click on "Videos" in the top tool bar, under the More pull-down menu, or from the left-side menu.

Figure 5.1 Google Videos search screen

Enter your search terms to find videos relevant to your need or interest, then press the Enter key or click the "Google Search" button (figure 5.2).

Google Videos crawls the web, looking for videos anywhere they may appear. Results will include links to websites that specifically host videos, such as YouTube and Vimeo, and web pages that happen to have videos embedded in them.

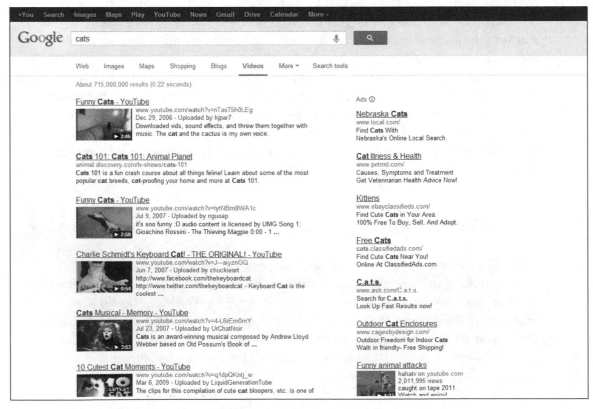

Figure 5.2 Google Videos search results for *cats*

Advanced Video Search

If you're still having trouble finding what you need, additional filtering is available via the Advanced Video Search page. As with most other Google search services, there is an advanced search option. However, finding it is a bit difficult, as a link to it is presented to you only at the bottom of a results page. Otherwise you can access it directly via the URL http://www.google.com/advanced_video_search (figure 5.3).

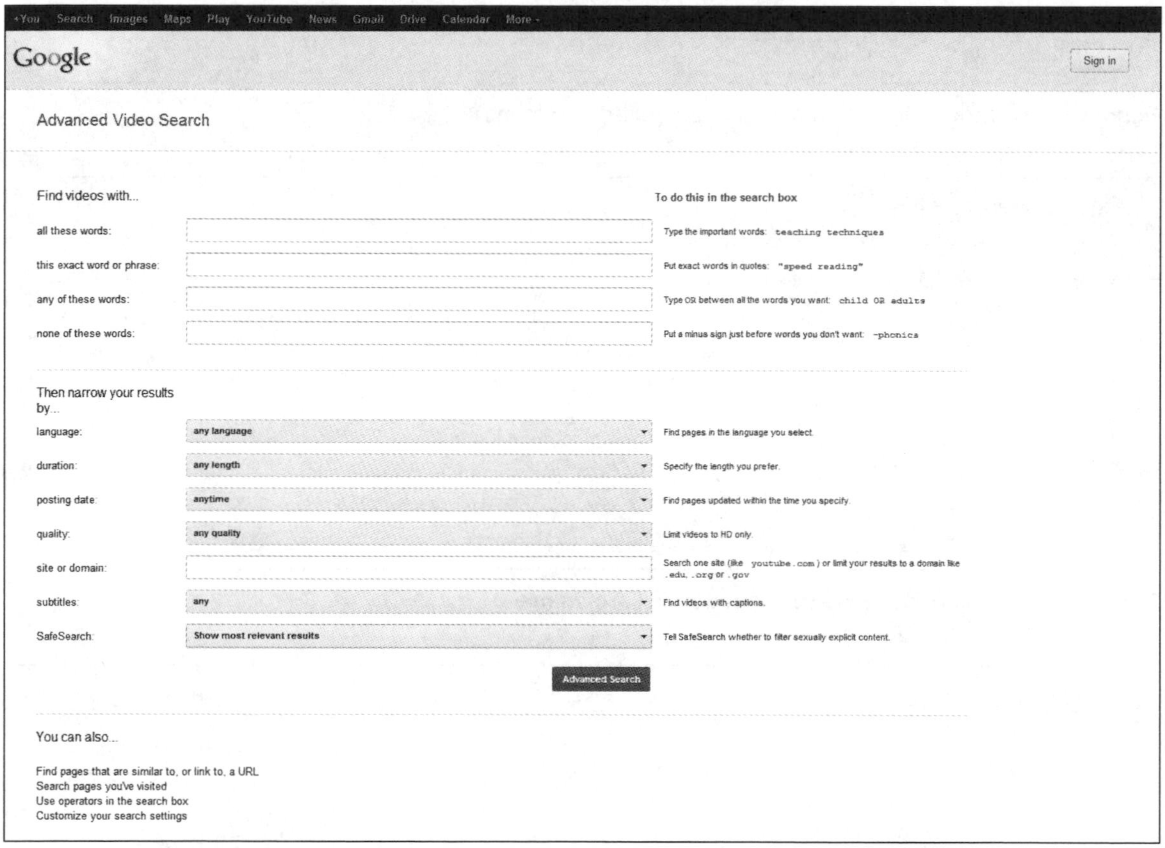

Figure 5.3 Advanced Video Search page

To start with, you will have the usual word limiting options. Following that are the video specific advanced searching options.

- Language—find pages in the language you select (figure 5.4).
- Duration—chose the length of video you prefer: any length, short (0–4 min.), medium (4–20 min.), or long (20+ min.) (figure 5.5).
- Posting date—limit your search to pages that have been updated anytime or in the past hour, past 24 hours, past week, past month, or past year (figure 5.6).

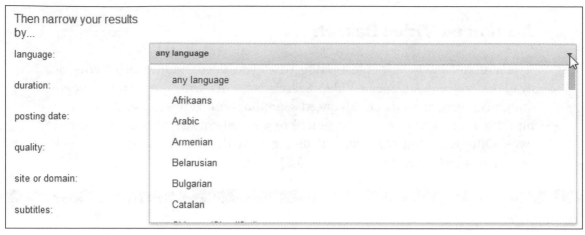

Figure 5.4 Advanced Video Search language pull-down menu

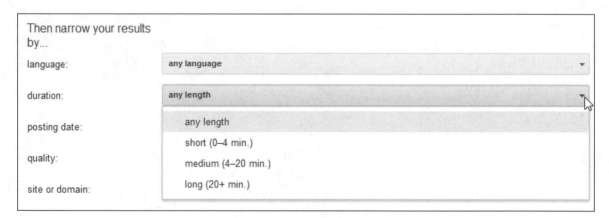

Figure 5.5 Advanced Video Search duration pull-down menu

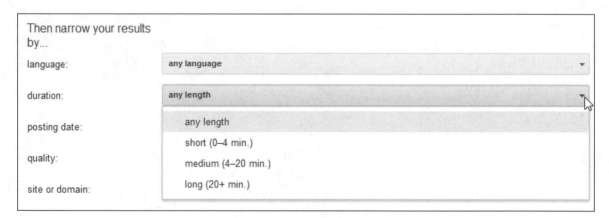

Figure 5.6 Advanced Video Search posting date pull-down menu

- Quality—choose between "any quality" and "HD only."
- Site or domain—enter a particular URL to search, or a certain domain, such as .gov or .org.
- Subtitles—find videos that have closed captioning.

Videos Search Results

The Google Videos search results page is arranged like most of the other search results pages. The search box, with your search terms included, is at the top, along with links related to your Google account and Google+ services. Just below this, the links to other types of searches are presented, followed by the Search tools link, which provides more search limiters. Next, you will find the number of results and the length of time it took Google to perform the search—and all the way to the right is the gear icon to access your general search settings, web history, and search help. If there are any Ads or Sponsored links, they will appear either at the top of your results and/or off to the right. At the bottom of the page are the standard next/previous page of results links and some suggested searches related to your search term(s).

STANDARD RESULT

Your standard Video search results list will show the most relevant match first, followed by the next relevant match, and so on. A typical Video result (figure 5.7) will include:

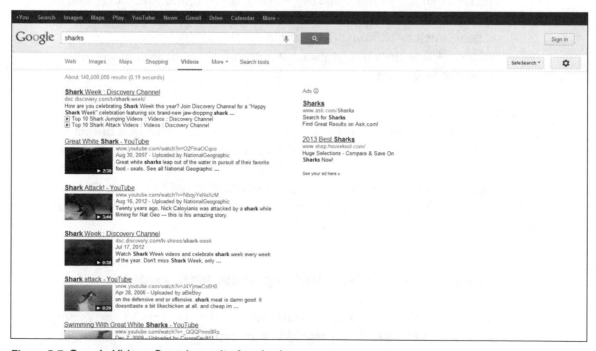

Figure 5.7 Google Videos Search results for *sharks*

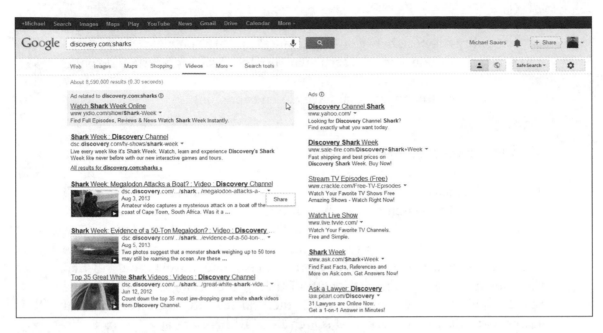

Figure 5.8 Navigation options from the Google Search results for *sharks*

- Title of the video: This is a hot link that you can click to go to the page with the video.
- URL: In green, you'll see the web address of the video.
- Date, Length, Uploaded by: Depending on what information Google can pull from the web page, the results will include the date on the video (when it was uploaded or created), the length of the video, and who uploaded the video—this could be a YouTube user name or a website, such as National Geographic.
- Snippet: A few lines of text excerpted from the description of the video on the web page.

At the end of the URL, you will see a green down arrow. Click it to get a drop-down menu with up to three options (figure 5.8). The first option is Cached, which will bring up the cached view of the page, a snapshot of the page as it appeared at a particular time. The second option is Similar, which will bring up a list of pages like that page. If you are logged in to your Google account, it will also show a Share option, so that you can share the result on Google+.

The Videos Search Results Options and Tools

You can further refine your search using the filtering options in the panel above your search results. If you would like to expand your search to other

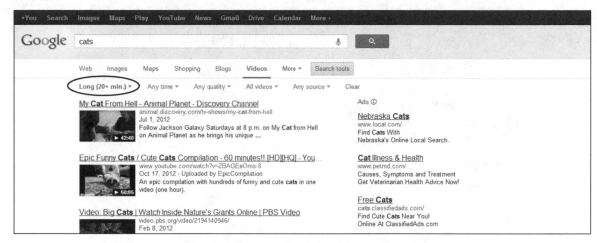

Figure 5.9 Google Videos search results for *cats*, limited to videos 20+ minutes long

types of content besides Videos, you can switch to see results such as Images or News. To see all types of content, choose "Web."

Click "Search tools" for the video-specific filters. The following pull-down menus will appear below the content options:

- *Duration*
  You can limit your search to videos of a certain length—Short (0–4 min.), Medium (4–20 min.), or Long (20+ min.) (figure 5.9). Click on "Any duration" to return to the full results list.

- *Time*
  Limit your results to videos posted during the following times: Past hour, Past 24 hours, Past week, Past month, or Past year; or with "Custom range . . ." you can enter specific dates (figure 5.10). Click on "Any time" to return to the full results list.

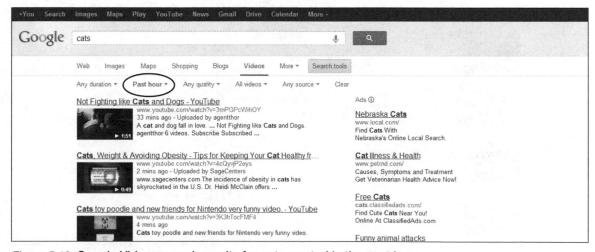

Figure 5.10 Google Videos search results for *cats*, posted in the past hour

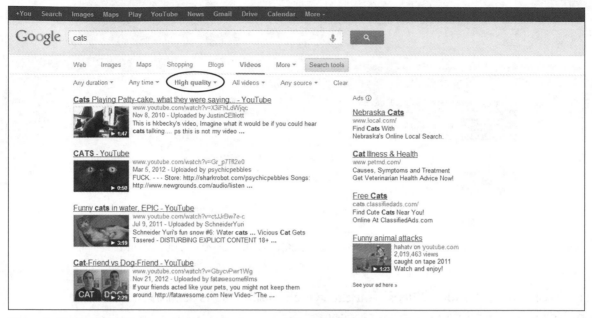

Figure 5.11 Google Videos search results for *cats,* HD videos only

- *Quality*
  Limit videos to HD only by choosing "High quality" (figure 5.11). Click "Any quality" to return to the full results list.

- *Subtitles*
  Find videos with closed captions by clicking "Closed captioned" (figure 5.12). Click "All videos" to return to the full results list.

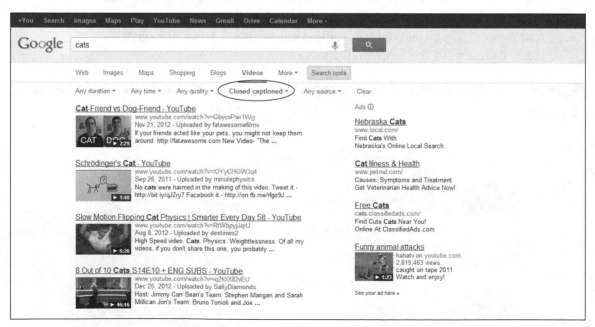

Figure 5.12 Google Videos search results for *cats* with closed captioning

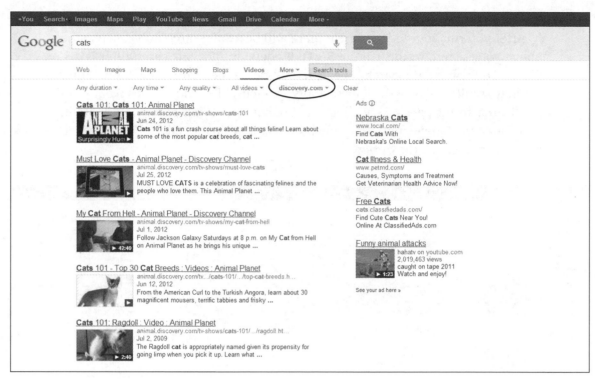

Figure 5.13 Google Images search results for *cats* on discovery.com

- *Source*
  Search one site, such as youtube.com, discovery.com, or ehow.com (figure 5.13). Click "Any source" to return to the full results list.

SafeSearch

Working in libraries, and with the public, you will often want or need to prevent objectionable adult videos from appearing in your search results. The results you see when you search in Google Video may contain mature content. Google considers a number of factors when determining whether a video is relevant to your search request. Because these methods aren't entirely foolproof, it's possible some inappropriate videos may be included among the videos you see.

SafeSearch allows you to change your browser settings to help eliminate videos that contain pornography or explicit sexual content. Again, no filter is perfect, but SafeSearch does a pretty good job of filtering out most objectionable content. To identify this content, Google uses automated algorithms that look at many factors, including keywords, links, and images.

After you run your video search, there will be a SafeSearch pull-down menu above your search results (figure 5.14). By default, the SafeSearch filter is disabled. To enable SafeSearch, open the pull-down menu, then click on "Filter explicit results." This will filter sexually explicit video and images from Google Search result pages, as well as results that might link to explicit content. To disable the SafeSearch filter, open the menu again and click "Filter explicit results" to uncheck the option.

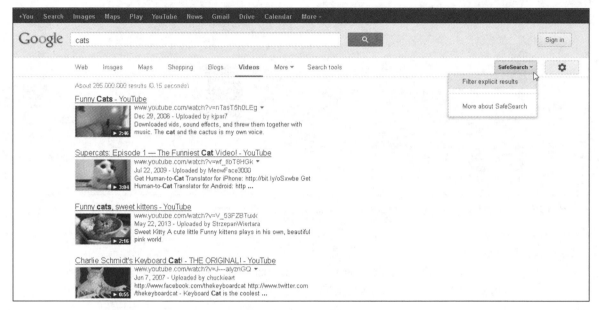

Figure 5.14 Google Videos search results SafeSearch pull-down menu

chapter 6

Google Maps

ONE OF THE most popular local search services today is Google Maps. You may have thought of it only as a place to get directions or look at satellite images for fun, but there are many features of Google Maps that can enhance your library's services and help your patrons. Although in many cases the features are built into the companies' main search engines (for example, if you include a zip code or "city, state" in a Google search you'll be presented with local results before web results), in this chapter, we focus on the local interfaces that Google Maps provides.

A Few Notes on the Google Map Interface

First-time users of map and local sites tend to quickly notice that these pages do not work the same as the more traditional web pages to which we've all become accustomed. To add to some users' frustration, the mouse doesn't always do what they expect. Before we get into searching Google Maps, we'd like to point out a few things that will save you a certain amount of frustration in the long run.

First, there are zooming controls located in the upper left corner of the map. These contain plus (zoom in) and minus (zoom out) buttons. There is also a slider bar on which you can drag a marker up or down to zoom in and out, respectively. Using these methods will zoom on the current center of the map.

However, when the mouse pointer is on the map, the mouse's scroll wheel also acts as a zoom controller, scrolling forward (away from you) to zoom in and scrolling back (toward you) to zoom out. Also, zooming with the scroll wheel tends to zoom in on the point where the mouse pointer currently is, not on the center of the map. When the mouse pointer is not on the map, the scroll wheel will act normally and scroll the page. Also, double-clicking the left mouse button while on the map will zoom in one level on wherever your pointer was, and double-clicking the right mouse button will zoom out one level.

At the top of the zooming controls, you will see a little yellow figure named "Pegman."[1] He is the Street View controller. With recent advances in technology and digital storage, companies such as Google are investing millions of dollars in bringing local search to the street level. Right now, this involves specially fitted vehicles driving through major metropolitan areas and photographing what they see every few feet. These photographs are then pieced together and rendered in the street view as if you were driving down the street yourself. To view street-level imagery in Google Maps, click and drag Pegman to the place you want to see. Roads with Street View imagery appear with a blue border (figure 6.1).

Figure 6.1 Google Maps street view of Las Vegas, Nevada

Second, when the mouse pointer hovers over a map, you can also drag the map in any direction within the display window. For example, for US-based users, Google Maps starts by showing the United States because that's where you are. If you want to see Europe, the easiest way is to move the mouse pointer over to the east (right) side of the map, press and hold down the left mouse button, and drag the map to the west (left) until you see Europe on the screen. Keep in mind that it may take a few seconds for the new areas of the map to load, so don't be worried if it looks like a part of the world has fallen off the map.

Third, a word of warning: avoid using your back button. Most map services are designed using newer coding methods, and despite what you do on the screen, you have not actually changed pages or gone "forward" to another page. When working on a map site for 15 or 20 minutes, you might click the back button only to end up on the page you were on before you went to the maps site. To get back to the map you were working on, you have to click forward and start all over again. In some cases, the back button will work, but it's better to get into the habit of not using it and using the in-page controls instead.

Lastly, Google Maps offers multiple views, called layers. The basic two are Map and Satellite. You can toggle between Map and Satellite views using the icon in the upper right corner of the map. Google Maps also offers other layers, such as "traffic," "weather," and "webcams." You may switch between these views by using the pull-down menu located in the upper-right corner of the map. Here's a brief description and example from Google Maps of each view.

- *Map*
  The map view shows a basic colored line-drawing map of the area. Streets are labeled, and one-way streets are indicated (figure 6.2).

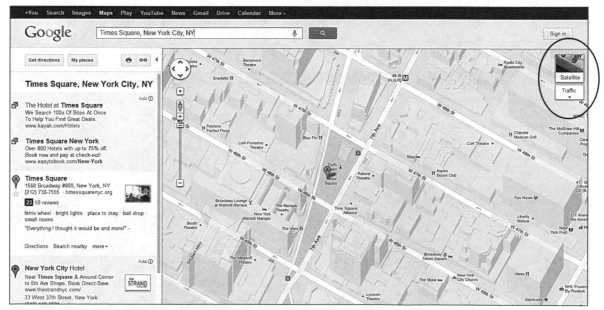

Figure 6.2 Google Maps map view of Times Square

Figure 6.3 Google Maps satellite view of Times Square

- *Satellite*
  The satellite view shows a combination of the map view and a photographic view of the area from above (figure 6.3). Satellite images can be as much as months or years out of date, and not all areas are covered. You can toggle off the map layer using Labels from the layers pull-down menu. This will give you the satellite view alone.

- *Terrain*
  The terrain view shows the 3D detailed terrain and elevation of the area (figure 6.4).

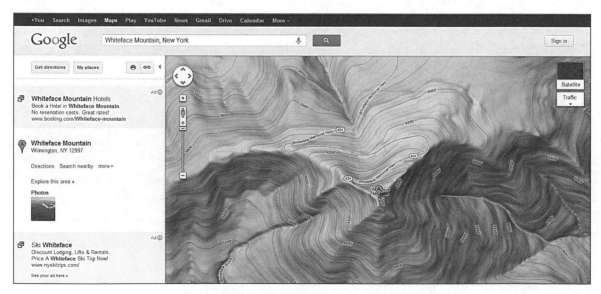

Figure 6.4 Google Maps terrain view of the Whiteface Mountain, New York area

Figure 6.5 Google Maps traffic view of Los Angeles, California

- *Traffic*

  When this button is available you can overlay real-time traffic speeds on your current view (figure 6.5). This typically works only for highways and color-codes the current speeds. In Google Maps the colors are "Green: more than 50 miles per hour," "Yellow: 25–50 miles per hour," "Red: less than 25 miles per hour," "Red/Black: very slow, stop-and-go traffic," and "Gray: no data currently available."

- *Photos*

  The photo layer shows photos taken from locations all around the world (figure 6.6). The photos come from Panoramio, Google's geolocation-oriented photo sharing website.

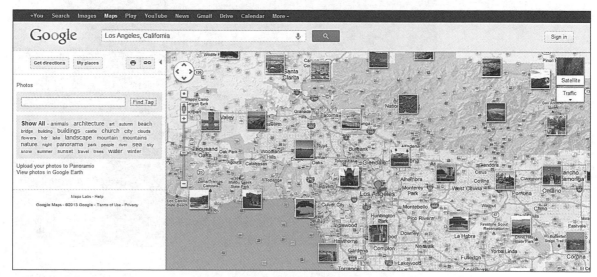

Figure 6.6 Google Maps photos view of Los Angeles, California

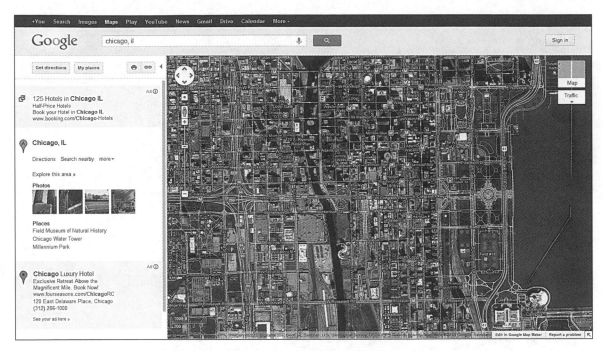

Figure 6.7 Google Maps satellite view with labels of Chicago, Illinois

- *Labels*
  The labels layer shows street, city, and boundary names within your
  map when in Satellite view (figure 6.7 and 6.8).

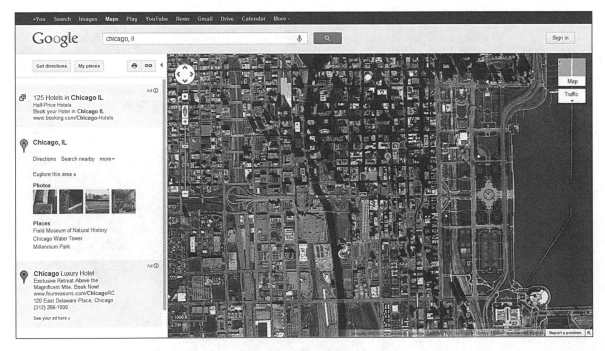

Figure 6.8 Google Maps satellite view without labels of Chicago, Illinois

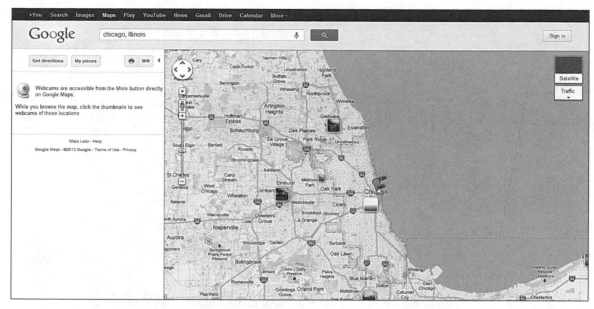

Figure 6.9 Google Maps webcams view of Chicago, Illinois

- *Webcams*
  With the webcams layer, you can view a snapshot taken from webcams within the last hour (figure 6.9). The webcams come from Webcams .travel, an online webcam community.

- *Weather*
  The weather layer shows weather conditions and forecasts from the Weather Channel. Temperature is available in both Fahrenheit and Celsius (figure 6.10). Satellite imagery of cloud cover can be toggled on and off.

Figure 6.10 Google Maps weather view of Seattle, Washington

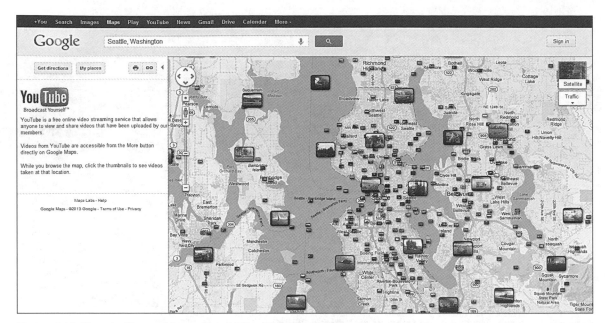

Figure 6.11 Google Maps videos view of Seattle, Washington

- *Videos*
  The videos layer allows you to watch geotagged[2] YouTube videos recorded from locations on the map (figure 6.11).

- *Wikipedia*
  The Wikipedia layer shows the beginning of geotagged Wikipedia articles (figure 6.12). A link to view the full article is provided.

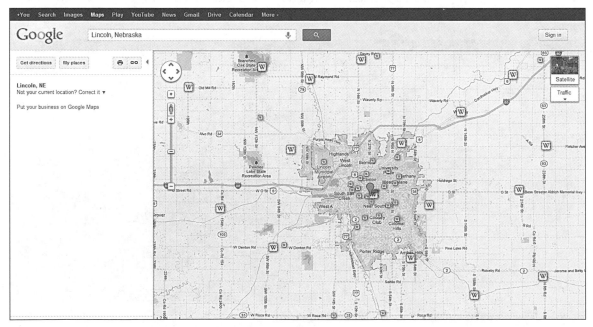

Figure 6.12 Google Maps Wikipedia view of Lincoln, Nebraska

Figure 6.13 Google Maps bicycling view of Lincoln, Nebraska

- *Bicycling*

  The bicycling layer shows biking paths and trails (figure 6.13). Three types of lines appear on the map: "Trails—dedicated bike-only trail," "Dedicated lanes—dedicated bike lane along a road," and "Bicycle friendly roads" (roads that are designated as preferred for bicycling, but without dedicated lanes). You can also get biking directions from Google Maps.

- *45°*

  The 45° layer shows select locations on the map at a 45° angle, birds'-eye view (figure 6.14). The images are taken from the air, so they are closer and crisper than the satellite images taken from orbit.

Figure 6.14 Google Maps 45° view of Las Vegas, Nevada

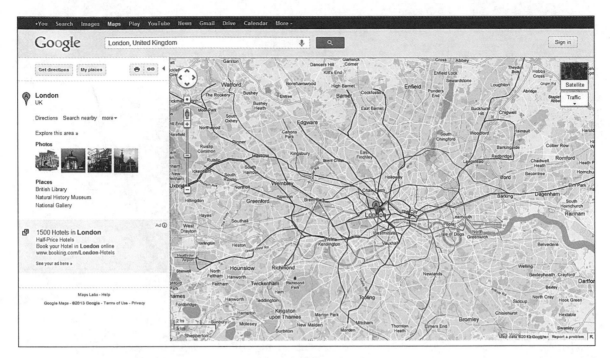

Figure 6.15 Google Maps transit view of London, United Kingdom

- *Transit*
  The transit layer allows you to see the public transport network of your city overlaid on the map (figure 6.15).

Getting Started

Today, Google Maps is the single interface to what used to be two separate searching interfaces: Google's mapping service and the Google Local searching service. You can use either http://maps.google.com or http://local.google .com to get to the service's home page, as shown in figure 6.16.

Once there you are presented with a map of the United States on which you can pan and zoom as described in the previous section. (Alternatively, if you're using a browser such as Chrome that has access to your location information, the map you are presented with is of your general area.) You can change this view to your immediate area by using the "Set default location" link. At the top of the page, you'll see a search box that you can use to search the interface. A "Get Directions" button is available on the top left.

Each of these represents a different method of searching Google Maps. Using the search box, you can actually change the method of your search through the way you type your search. For example, typing an address will do a map search, while typing two addresses with the word *to* between them will do a

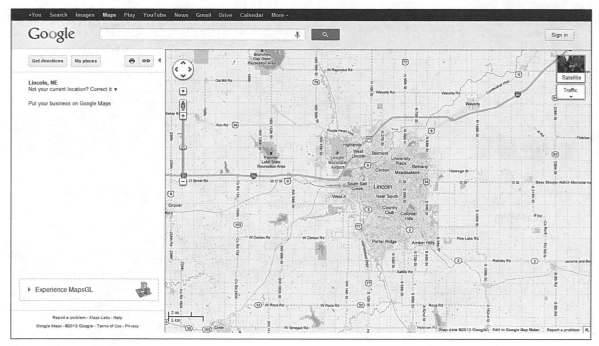

Figure 6.16 Google Maps web page

directions search. However, for simplicity's sake, let's take a look at a location search, a business search, and a search for driving directions.

LOCATION SEARCH

A map search is designed to accept a location as your search term. A location can be formatted in a number of different ways. For example:

- Zip code (68508; figure 6.17)
- City, state (Lincoln, NE; figure 6.18)
- Street and zip code (1200 N St, 68508; figure 6.19)
- A full address (301 N 12th St, Lincoln, NE 68508; figure 6.20)

Entering your search in any of these four formats will return to you a single match with the map zoomed in to the appropriate level with a marker on the location of your result. Clicking on the marker brings up a balloon with a brief description of your result and links for more options—Directions, Search nearby, and Save to map. You can close this balloon by clicking the "x" in its upper-right corner.

If you type in what Google considers to be an incomplete location—for example, just a street address but not a city/state or zip code, the first thing it will do is look for that address in the same geographic area of your last search. For example, if you've recently searched for locations in Lincoln, Nebraska, a search for *1200 o st* will retrieve that address in Lincoln, Nebraska (figure 6.21).

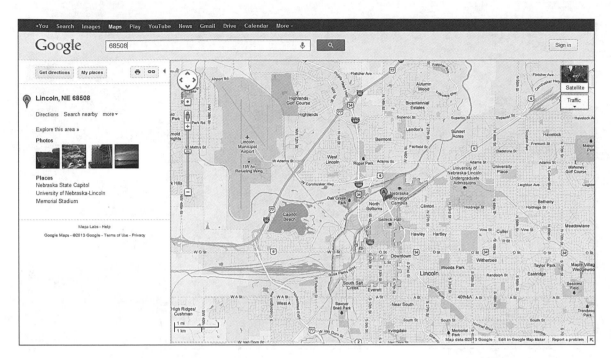

Figure 6.17 Zip code search results

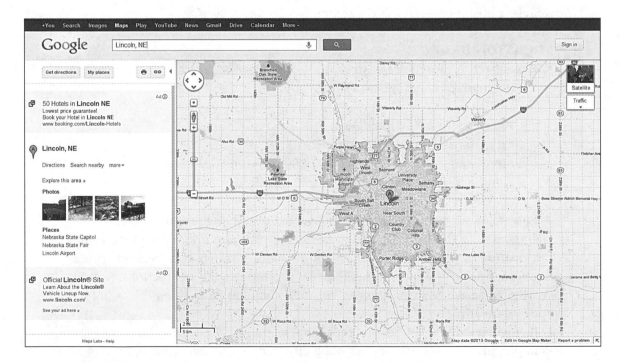

Figure 6.18 City, State search results

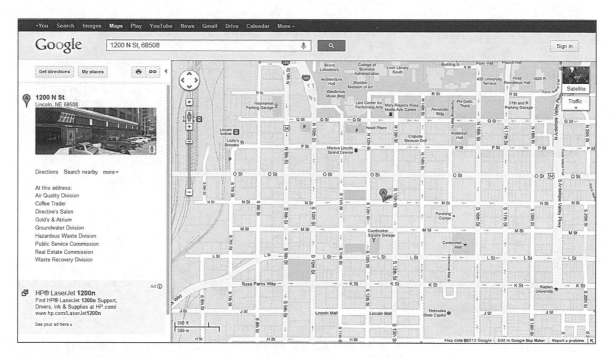

Figure 6.19 Street and zip code search results

Figure 6.20 Full address search results

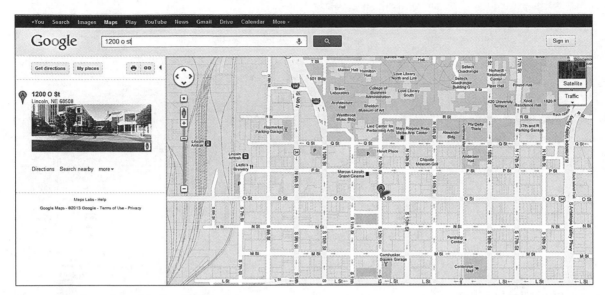

Figure 6.21 Search results for *1200 o st*

However, if you were to search for *10 bellevue st*, Google will not find any such address in the Lincoln, Nebraska, area and will return a list of possible results from a much larger search area—in this case, Bellevue Street in Jena, Louisiana (figure 6.22).

Using the "current location" option, which appears when you first access Google Maps, makes the process work a little more smoothly. For example, if you set your default location to Lincoln, Nebraska, whenever you come back to Google Maps, the map will start with that location, and any searches you do will assume that you're looking for things within the Lincoln area first. If the current location setting isn't correct, use the "Not your current location? Correct it" option to enter a new location (figure 6.23).

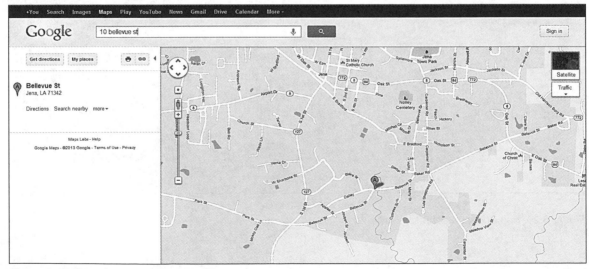

Figure 6.22 Search results for *10 bellevue st*

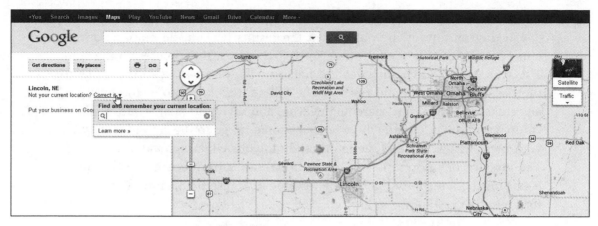

Figure 6.23 Set default location: Lincoln, Nebraska

BUSINESS SEARCH

If you don't have any address information, you can search for a type of business or a specific business in a particular area. For example, say your patron is looking for a good Indian restaurant in town. In this case you would enter *indian* and your general location (city, state, and/or zip code.) If you don't specify one, your current location will automatically be used as the location for the business search. You can change this if it isn't appropriate for your search.

Your results are presented to you in groups of ten to the left of the map, as seen in figure 6.24. Each result is labeled with a letter: A–J for the first ten, K–T for the next ten, and so on, which will match a lettered pointer on the map.

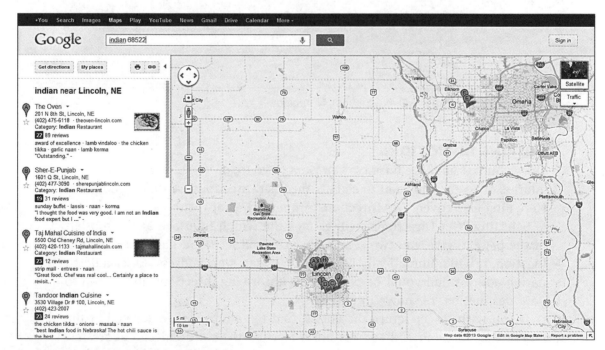

Figure 6.24 Search for a business results

Clicking on any of the pointers in the results list, on the map, or on the name of a result will open the descriptive balloon for that pointer on the map. The balloon generally includes the name of the business, a rating, links to the business's website and reviews, the full address, a photo of the business, and links for directions, searching nearby, and saving to map. There is also a "More" pull-down menu, where you can zoom in, go to the street view, write your own review, or send the information to your e-mail, phone, car, or GPS. The amount of information in this balloon varies from business to business based on the information available to Google. Figure 6.25 shows the balloon for an Indian restaurant in Lincoln, Nebraska: The Oven.

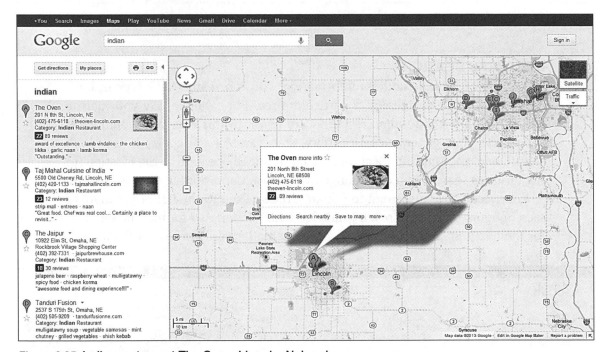

Figure 6.25 Indian restaurant The Oven, Lincoln, Nebraska

DRIVING DIRECTIONS

Once you've found the business you want to go to, or if you already know the address of where you want to end up, the "Get Directions" search is your final step. First let's cover "Get Directions" from the link at the top.

Selecting "Get Directions" will change the search interface at the top left of the page to give you two search boxes, A and B. If you have set a default location, it will automatically be filled in as your start address. Enter a destination address and you'll be presented with driving directions and a map to your destination, as shown in figure 6.26.

If you wish to get return directions, find the double arrow located at the end of the start and end address fields to swap the start and end addresses. Click the arrow and the directions reverse. This is also handy if you wish to

Figure 6.26 Directions from Lincoln, Nebraska, to Homer Glen, Illinois

get directions from your first destination to a second destination: perform the switch, then type in a new end address.

Once you have your route, you have a few options for customizing it. First click on the "Show options" link under box B. You can check the "Avoid highways" option if you would like a more scenic route, as shown in figure 6.27.

Second, if you wish to stop in a particular location that isn't included on the route that Google provides, you can drag a spot on the blue route line to the location you wish to include, thereby changing the route. As a result, the directions

Figure 6.27 Customizing directions to avoid highways

Figure 6.28 Directions from Lincoln, Nebraska, to Homer Glen, Illinois, with a stop in Waterloo, Iowa

will be updated accordingly. For example, figure 6.28 shows the route from Lincoln, Nebraska, to Homer Glen, Illinois, with a stop in Waterloo, Iowa. You can click the "Add Destination" link, which provides additional search boxes (box C, box D, etc., up to box Y) for directions to stops along the way.

These last options can be most useful when planning a multi-destination trip. Start by finding the directions from your start to the furthest location, and then customize (drag) your route to include the additional places where you wish to stop, or enter the extra stops into the extra "Add Destination" boxes (figure 6.29). If on your return trip you wish to take a completely different route, just reverse the directions and move your route accordingly.

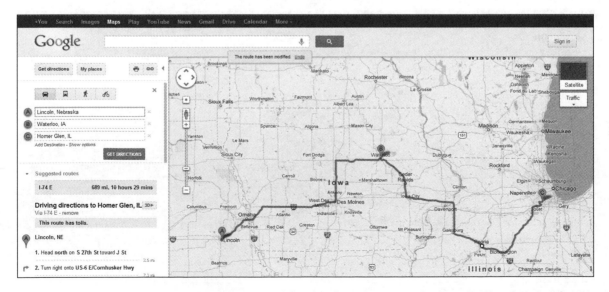

Figure 6.29 Directions from Lincoln, Nebraska, to Homer Glen, Illinois, with stops in Waterloo, Iowa, and Peoria, Illinois (via dragging the route)

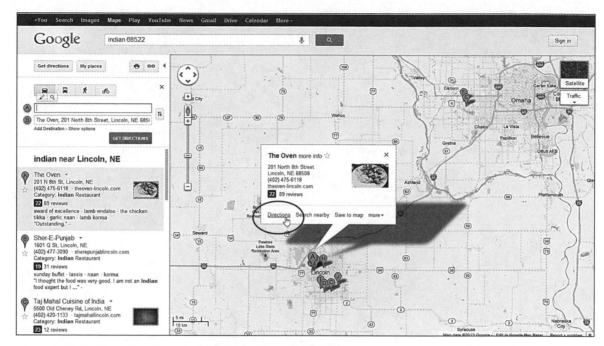

Figure 6.30 Getting directions to The Oven, Lincoln, Nebraska

As you may have noticed, if you're on a balloon for a particular location, you can click on "Directions" in the balloon to also access this search. When you select "Directions" in a balloon, it will give you a start address box (with your default location presupplied if you've set one), as shown in figure 6.30. This assumes that you're traveling to that location. If you wish to get directions from that location, click on the double arrow located at the end of the start and end address fields to swap the addresses.

OUTPUT OPTIONS

Once you have chosen the map view that works best for you (see earlier in this chapter), you need to choose which output method you wish to use. Your choices are "Print" or "Link." Link includes the ability to "Send."

Print

Whether you have a map of an area, the location of a business, or directions from point A to point B, you're most likely going to want a printed copy. Unfortunately, what you're looking at on the screen is oriented in landscape format (especially if you're using a widescreen monitor) and by default, your printer prints portrait. The best way to handle this is not to use the print button built into your browser. Instead, use the print button located above the directions on the left. This will open a new window for you, formatted for the correct orientation, with a map that correctly fits on an 8.5-by-11 piece of paper in portrait format. Figures 6.31 and 6.32 show the print results for an area and a business.

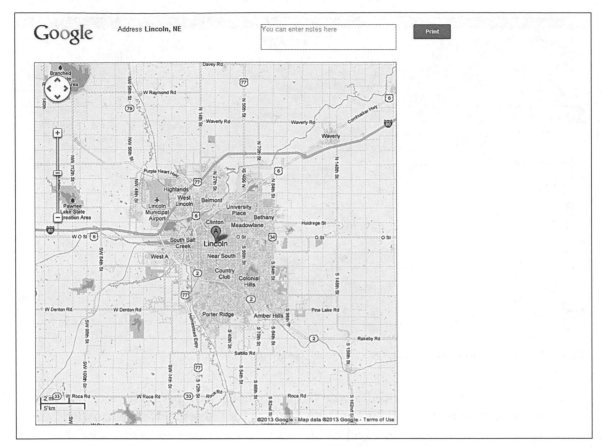

Figure 6.31 Print results for a location

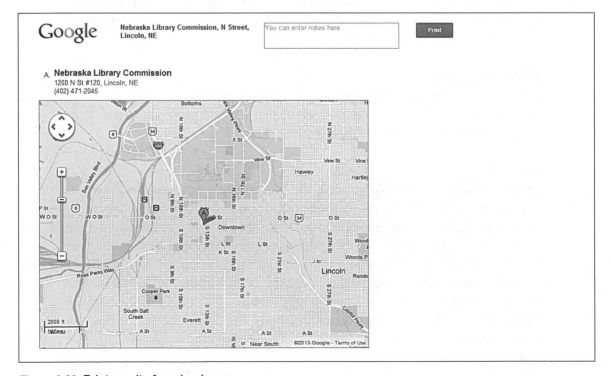

Figure 6.32 Print results for a business

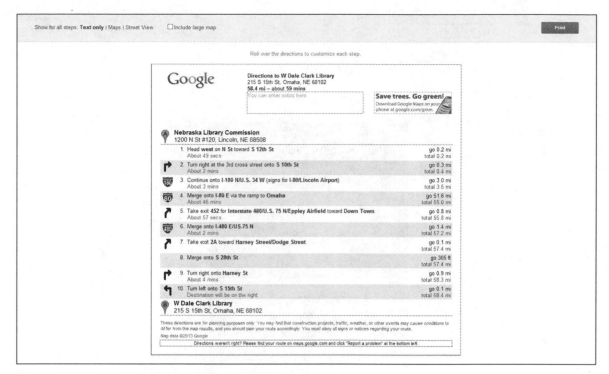

Figure 6.33 Print output of directions: text only

Figures 6.33 through 6.36 show the print views for directions. The three main print views are "Text only" (figure 6.33); "Maps," which will show a map for each turn (figure 6.34); and "Street view," which will display images of the area as if you were looking out your car window, if available (figure 6.35). In addition, you can check the "Include large map" option on any of these three views to have a trip overview map included at the beginning of your printout (figure 6.36).

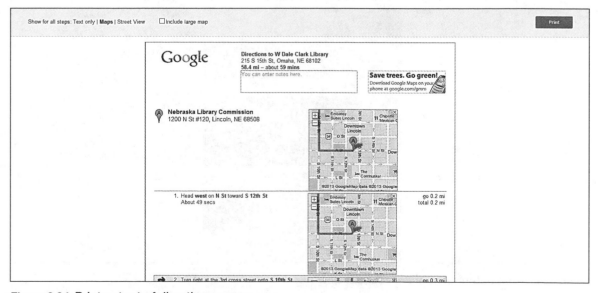

Figure 6.34 Print output of directions: maps

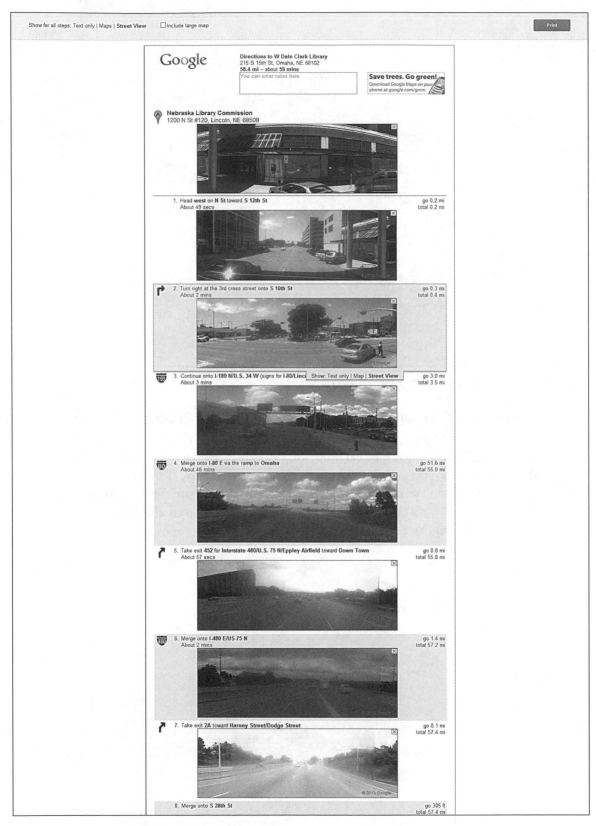

Figure 6.35 Print output of directions: street view

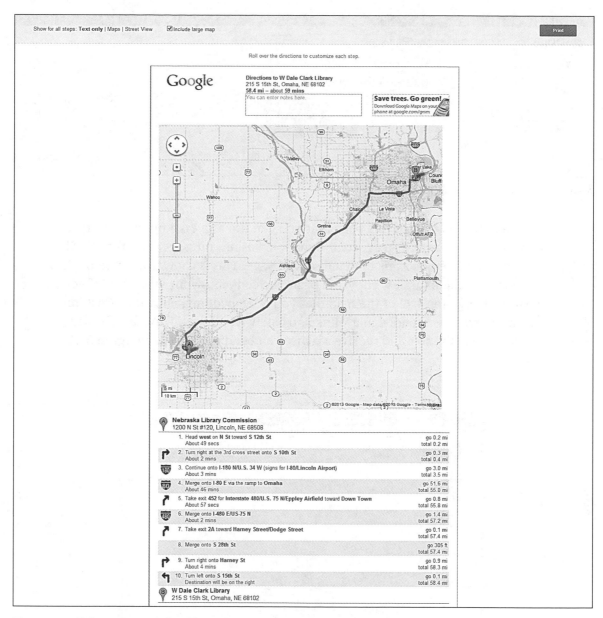

Figure 6.36 Print output of directions: text only including large map

Link

Because of the nature of the technology running Google Maps, the URL of the page does not change all that often while you're navigating the site. (This is why we suggest not using the browser's back button while searching these sites.) As a result, bookmarking what you're looking at or attaching the URL of your map in a regular e-mail is rather difficult. To do either of these things, you first need the real URL of what's on the screen. To get this, click on the "Link" button next to the "Print" button. This will give you two pieces of

Figure 6.37 Link information for directions

information: the URL of this page that you can use as a bookmark or paste as a hyperlink in a web page, regular e-mail, or instant message; and the HTML code needed to embed this map into a web page. This is shown in figure 6.37.

To embed the map, just copy and paste the code into your web page. If you wish to change the size of the map that you're embedding, click the "Customize and preview embedded map" link and a new window will appear, allowing you to change the size and receive a revised embedding code, as in figure 6.38.

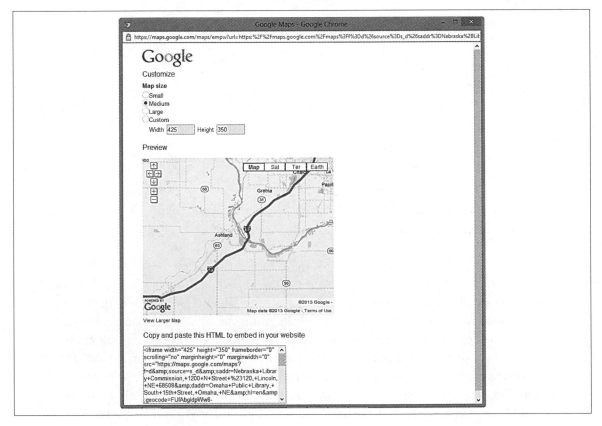

Figure 6.38 Customize embedded map

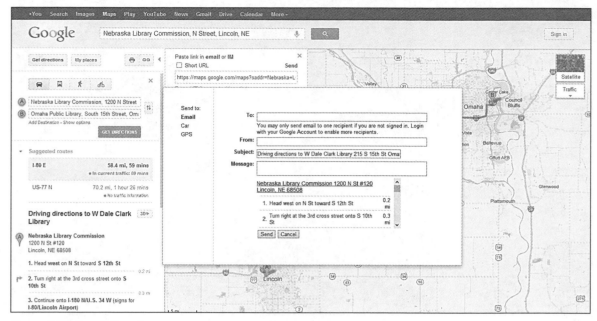

Figure 6.39 Send directions

Send

The Send option is great for when your patron is not in front of you but has e-mail access. In the upper right corner of the Link window is a Send link. When you click "Send," a window will appear on your screen, as in figure 6.39, with options to send to Email, Car, or GPS. To send to a patron's e-mail address, you are provided with the To and From e-mail address fields, and a message including a link to the map you're viewing. You can add additional text to the body of the message if you wish. Just fill out the form and send.

My Places

(For this section you will need to sign in to a Google account in order to take advantage of these features.)

If you find yourself regularly giving out the same map-based information or wish to create a highly detailed map that you can access in the future, choose the "My Places" option. The simplest way to use this feature is first to perform your search and customizations, and then click on the "My Places" button above the search results. Click the "Create map" button, give your map a title and a description, and then click the "Done" button (figure 6.40). Once you've done this, your map is now listed and easily retrievable from your list in the future. (For more details on creating custom maps, be sure to click on the "Explore making custom maps in an interactive tutorial" link available once you've clicked "My Places."

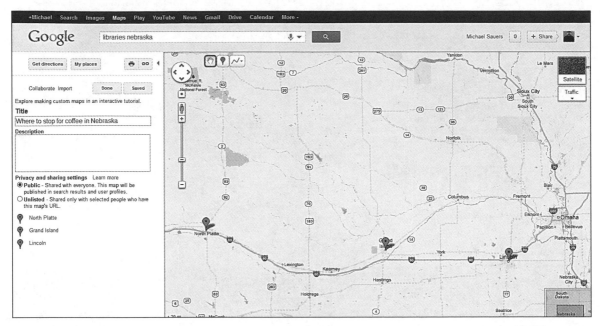

Figure 6.40 Create a map

SAVED LOCATIONS

One thing Google Maps does (without explicitly telling you) is to make a list of all your searched-for locations. You may have noticed that when you go into "My places," there is a list of the locations you found during your recent searches (figure 6.41).

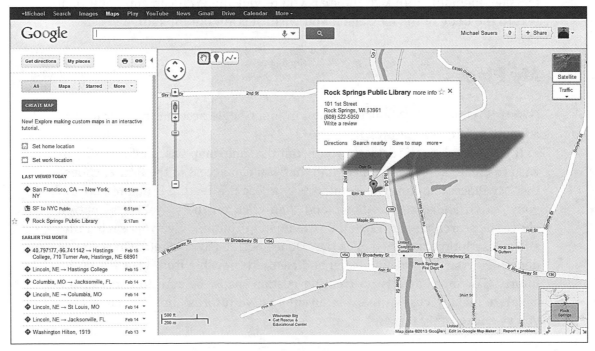

Figure 6.41 My places

By clicking on the name of a location in this list, you'll be taken to a map of that location. To delete content, click on the drop-down arrow to the right of any item and choose "Delete" from the pull-down menu. On the next page, click the "Delete" button to confirm that you want to delete this location from your search history.

Conclusion

Questions involving directions or "Where can I find service X in town?" are commonly asked in libraries. In the past, the yellow pages and maps have been the reference librarian's tools for answering these questions. Unfortunately, and in most cases, the patron isn't allowed to take these resources from the library. Now with services such as Google Maps, nearly any local resource can be found swiftly. Directions from the patron's location to the resource can be quickly created and a simple printout or e-mail can be sent with a minimal amount of effort.

NOTES

1. "Who is Pegman?" http://www.google.com/help/maps/streetview/learn/pegman.html.
2. "Geotagging," http://en.wikipedia.org/wiki/Geotagging.

$\mathcal{Q}$

Google Blog Search

BLOGS ARE COMMONPLACE on the Web today. The ability to search only blog posts can be very valuable to librarians and their patrons. Google Blog Search is a search technology focused on blogs. It can help you find out what bloggers have to say on any topic you research: book reviews, politics, recipes, or anything else you may need.

Google Blog Search indexes blogs by their RSS feeds, which are checked frequently for new content. Because of this, Blog Search results can update with new content more quickly than other types of Google searches. Also, because site feeds index individual posts and dates, more specific searches can be run with Blog Search.

Blogs created on any service are indexed: Blogger, WordPress, TypePad, and so on. As long as a blog publishes a site feed, Google Blog Search should be able to find it.

Basic Searching

You can get to Google Blog Search at http://www.google.com/blogsearch, as shown in figure 7.1. You can also search on the main Google page. When you do your search on Google.com, blogs and blog posts may be included in your search results. You can also click on "Blogs" in the top tool bar, under the "More" pull-down menu, or from the left-side menu.

Figure 7.1 Google Blog Search screen

Enter your search terms to find blogs or blog posts relevant to your need or interest, then press the Enter key or click the "Google Search" button.

Google Blog Search can return search results of both specific posts and entire blogs. If there are entire blogs that seem to be a good match for your search terms, these appear in a short list just above the main search results. Just above that list is a link to "Blog homepages" for your search terms. Click this link to bring up only results that are entire blogs (figure 7.2). To switch back to a combination of blogs and blog posts, click the "X" in the "Homepages" bar at the top of your new results list.

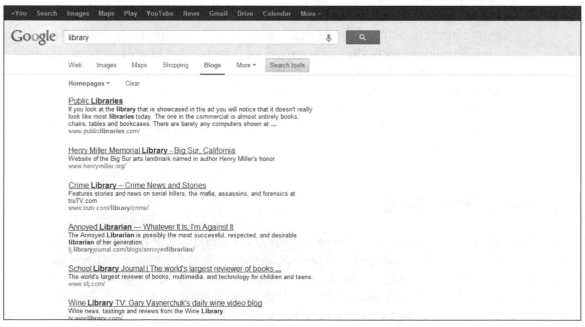

Figure 7.2 Google Blog Search results—homepages

Advanced Blog Search

If you're still having trouble finding what you need, additional limiting is available via the Advanced Search page for Google Blog Search. Click on the gear icon in the upper-right corner of your Blog results page. From the pull-down menu, choose "Advanced Search" (figure 7.3).

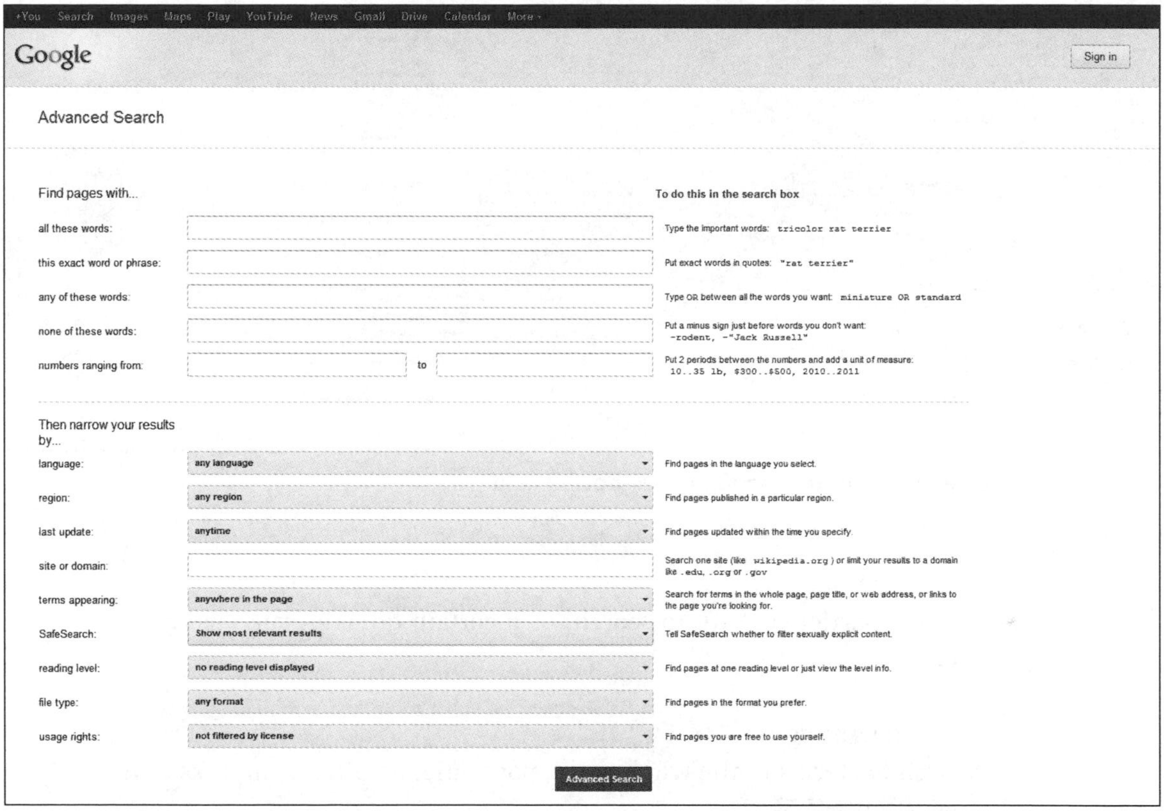

Figure 7.3 Advanced Blog Search screen

To start with, you will have the usual word limiting options that were covered in chapter 1. Following that are the blog-specific advanced searching options.

- *Language*
  Find pages in the language you select (figure 7.4).

- *Region*
  Search for images geographically, using the pull-down menu to choose a country.

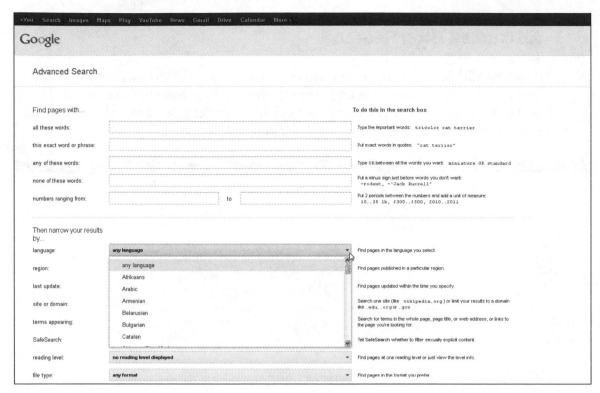

Figure 7.4 Advanced Blog Search language pull-down menu

- *Site or domain*
  Enter a particular URL to search, or a certain domain, such as .gov or .org.

- *Terms appearing*
  Search for terms in the whole page, page title, or URL, or in links to the page (figure 7.5).

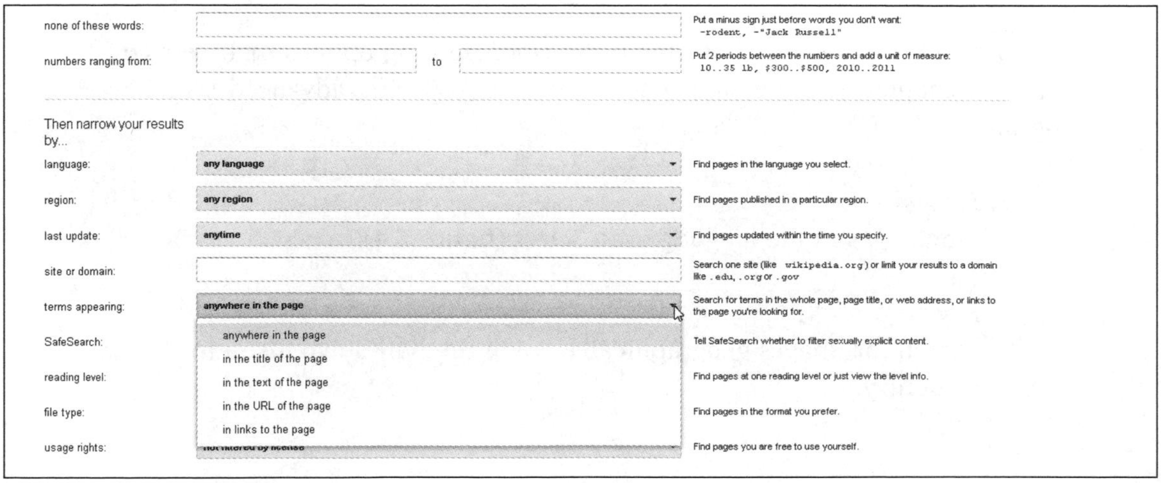

Figure 7.5 Advanced Search terms pull-down menu

- *SafeSearch*

  This setting allows you to change your browser settings to help eliminate adult content from your search results. By default, the SafeSearch filter is disabled. To enable SafeSearch, open the pull-down menu, then click on "Filter explicit results." This will filter sexually explicit video and images from Google Search result pages, as well as results that might link to explicit content. To disable the SafeSearch filter, open the menu again and click "Show most relevant results."

- *Reading level*

  Here you can limit your search results to a specific reading level: Basic, Intermediate, or Advanced. You can also choose to see results annotated with reading levels, which includes a percentage breakdown of results by reading level (figure 7.6).

- *File type*

  Here you can limit your results to pages in a particular format—.pdf, .xls, .ppt, .doc, and so on.

- *Usage rights*

  As we've mentioned, if you are planning to reuse someone else's content from the web, it's always a good idea to check the usage rights

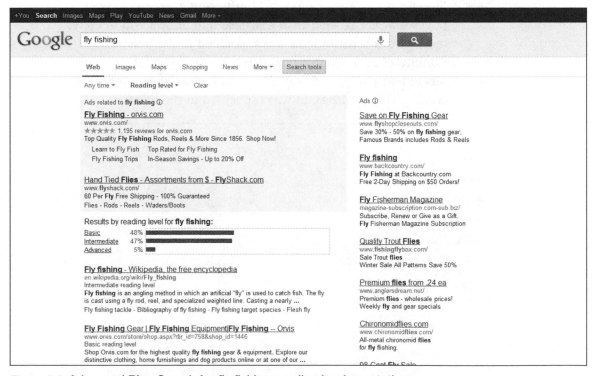

Figure 7.6 Advanced Blog Search for *fly fishing*, reading level annotation

that the original owner may have placed on their pages. The Advanced Blog Search usage rights filter can help you find content that you are allowed to use. The usage rights filter shows you pages that are either labeled with a Creative Commons license or labeled as being in the public domain. Creative Commons (http://creativecommons.org), a project started by Lawrence Lessig, allows content creators to assign a copyright-like license to their content, controlling attribution, commercial usage, and derivative creation. Once created, this license can be attached to the content, allowing users to know what permissions they do and do not have when it comes to using that content.

Before you use any content you find, you should check the actual license information on the original page. The Google Blog Search usage rights filter can help you get started, but it should not be the only research you do before using someone else's content.

The usage rights filtering options are shown in figure 7.7:

- Not filtered by license—limits your search results to pages on which Google could find no license or public domain indication.
- Free to use or share—limits your search results to pages that are either labeled as public domain or carry a license that allows you to copy or redistribute its content, as long as the content remains unchanged.
- Free to use, share, or modify—limits your search results to pages that are labeled with a license that allows you to copy, modify, or redistribute in ways specified in the license.
- Commercially—Limits your search results to pages that are labeled with a license that allows you to use the content for commercial purposes, in ways specified in the license.

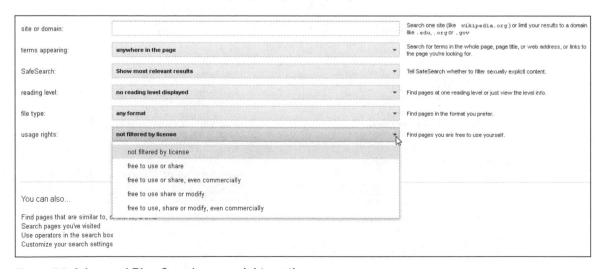

Figure 7.7 Advanced Blog Search usage rights options

Blog Search Results

The Blog search results page is similar to the other search results pages, but with one difference: no Ads or Sponsored links. Everything else remains the same. The search box, with your search terms included, is at the top, along with links related to your Google account and Google+ services. Just below this, the links to other types of searches are presented, followed by the Search tools link, which provides more search limiters. Next, you will find the number of results and the length of time it took Google to perform the search—and all the way to the right is the gear icon to access your general search settings, advanced search options, and web history. At the bottom of the page are the standard next/previous page of results links and some suggested searches related to your search term(s).

STANDARD RESULT

Your standard Blog search results list will show the blog search results first, followed by the specific blog post results. They will be in order of relevance, with the most relevant match first, followed by the next relevant match, and so on (figure 7.8). Both types of results include:

- Title of the blog or blog post: This is a hot link that you can click to go to the page where the blog or individual blog post is.
- URL: In green, you'll see the web address of the blog.

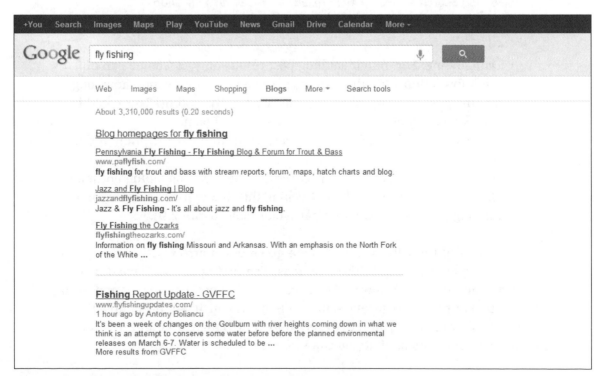

Figure 7.8 Google Blog Search results for *fly fishing*

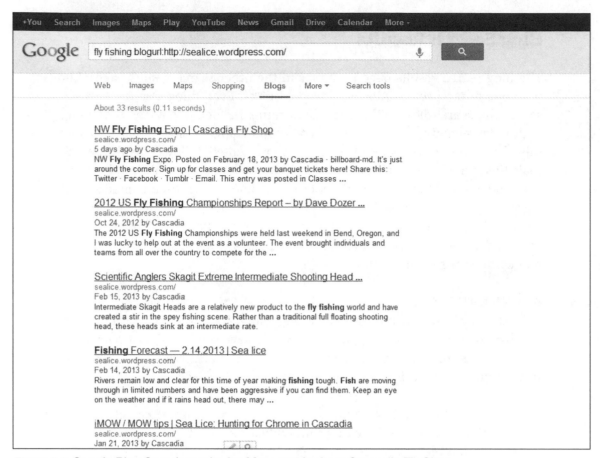

Figure 7.9 Google Blog Search results for *More results from Cascadia Fly Shop*

- Date, Byline: For individual blog post results only, if Google can pull the information from the web page, the results will include how long ago the post was published and the name of the author. This could be a screen name, not necessarily a blogger's real name.
- Snippet: A few lines of text are excerpted from the description of the blog or from the blog post itself.
- More results: For some blog post results, there will be a blue hotlink to "More results" from the blog. Clicking this link will run a new search for blog posts from only that particular blog (figure 7.9).

At the end of the URL, you will see a green down arrow. Click it to get a drop-down menu with up to three options. The first option is Cached, which will bring up the cached view of the page, a snapshot of the page as it appeared at a particular time. The second option is Similar, which will bring up a list of pages like that page. If you are logged in to your Google account, it will also show a Share option, so that you can share the result on Google+.

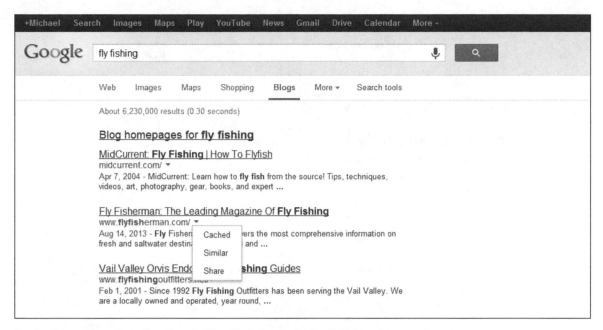

Navigation options from the Google Blog Search results for *fly fishing* blog post

Search Results Options and Tools

You can further refine your search by using the filtering options in the panel above your search results. If you would like to expand your search to other types of content besides Blogs, you can switch to see results such as Images or Videos. Click "More" to see all of the options. To see all types of content, choose "Web."

Click "Search tools" for even more ways to limit your results. The following blog-specific pull-down menus will appear below the content options:

- *Posts or home pages*
  This is another place where you can toggle your search results list between entire blogs, using the "Homepages" link, and a combination of blogs and blog posts (figure 7.11).

- *Time*
  Limit your results to blogs posted during the following times: Past 10 minutes, Past hour, Past 24 hours, Past week, Past month, Past year, or with "Custom range . . ." you can enter specific dates (figure 7.12). Click on "Any time" to return to the full results list.

- *Relevance or date*
  You can choose to sort your search results with the most relevant or the most recent at the top (figure 7.13).

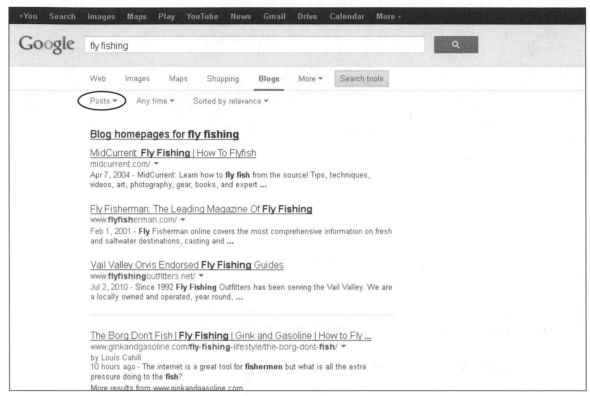

Figure 7.11 Google Blog Search results for *fly fishing*, limited to blog posts only

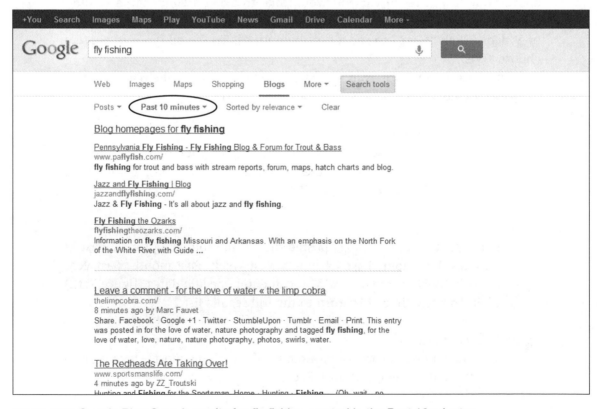

Figure 7.12 Google Blog Search results for *fly fishing*, posted in the Past 10 minutes

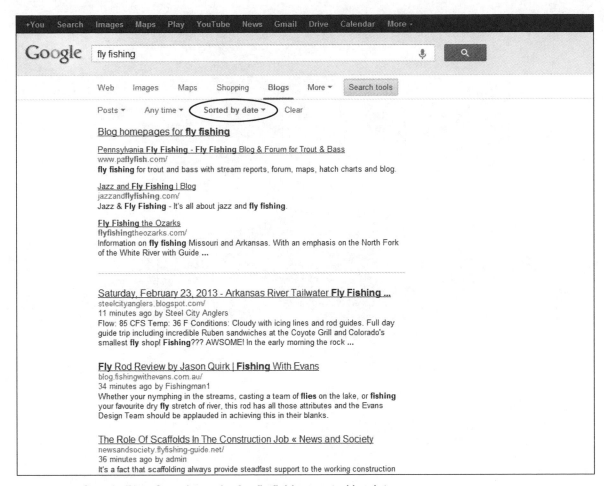

Figure 7.13 Google Blog Search results for *fly fishing,* sorted by date

Google Scholar

"STAND ON THE shoulders of giants" is the text that appears below the search field on the home page of Google Scholar. (http://scholar.google.com) Where most Google searches focus on finding web-based content regardless of the source, Google Scholar takes a significantly different approach and mainly deals with "scholarly" and other reviewed content, such as journal articles, dissertations, book publications, and other professional articles. If you're looking for more "traditional" research sources or if a teacher insists that sources cited "may not be just another website," this is the source for you.

One note before we get started: Google Scholar does allow you to cross-search both scholarly content and patents. Since Google has a separate patent search interface, we cover patent searching in chapter 9.

Basic Search

As soon as you open the Google Scholar search page (http://scholar.google .com) you'll notice that there's a bit more on the screen than on most of the other Google Search pages (figure 8.1). Up at the top right are links to My Citations (not covered in this book), Metrics, Alerts and Settings. We cover the latter three later in this chapter. Below the search box there are options to search Articles and/or patents (both selected by default) or Legal Documents. (Searching of patents will not be covered in this chapter as there is a separate patent search interface covered in chapter 9.)

Figure 8.1 Google Scholar basic search screen with default settings

To perform a basic search, enter your keywords in the search box, select whether you wish to search Articles or Legal Documents, and click the blue button with the magnifying glass. When we get to the results screen later in this chapter, we'll discuss how exactly what you're searching differs between Articles and Legal Documents.

Advanced Search

Similar to what is available in Google News, the advanced Scholar search has been integrated into the basic search interface instead of being presented on a page of its own. To find the advanced search features, click on the down-pointing triangle in the far right of the search box. This will bring up the advanced search options immediately below the search box. (See figure 8.2.)

As with most other advanced searches in Google, you're first presented with the standard advanced options: with **all** of the words, with **the exact phrase**, with **at least one** of the words, and **without** the words.

Next you'll see the Google Scholar–specific options:

- *Where my words occur*
  Here you can choose to limit your keywords to appearing "anywhere in the article" (default) or only "in the title of the article."

- *Return articles by*
  Enter names here to specify that they must appear somewhere in the author field. Use quotes to tie together first and last names (example: *"michael sauers"*) or just enter multiple names to have them all be

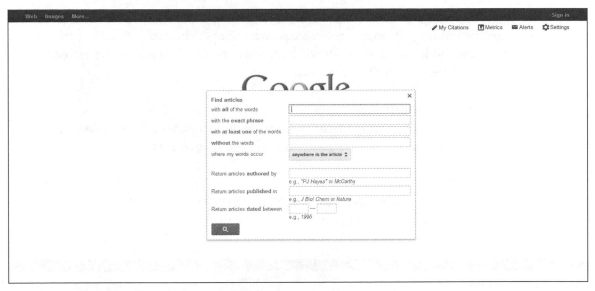

Figure 8.2 Google Scholar's advanced search features

searched for (example: *burns sauers*). It is not recommended that you search in a lastname, firstname format, as most authors will not be listed that way.

- *Return articles in*
  Enter the name of the publication you're looking for here. This especially works well when searching for articles. Example: *nature*

- *Return articles dated between*
  Use these two fields to specify a starting and/or ending date range for your search. Only years are accepted here. Example: 1990–1999

Once you have filled in the appropriate fields, click the blue search button to initiate your search.

Results

Once you have done a search, you can easily switch between the results of an article search or a legal document search through links in the Scholar toolbelt. The contents of the toolbelt will differ depending on the type of search results you are viewing. However, the presentation of the search results are generally the same between the two types of results. We cover the similar information in this section and the differences in the next.

Figure 8.3 shows the results of searching for *librarianship* as an article search. Figure 8.4 shows the results for the same search as a legal document search. As you can see, the results themselves, while different in actual content, are generally presented in the same way. For each result you are provided (as available) with the following information (with some of the latter items perhaps beneath a "More ▾" link:

- *The title of the article*
  This is the title of the article or legal document that is hyperlinked to the article's web page from the source listed below. If an online version is not available, the title will not be hyperlinked.

  - possibly preceded by [CITATION] [BOOK] [HTML] [PDF]
    However, if the title is preceded by [CITATION] then the

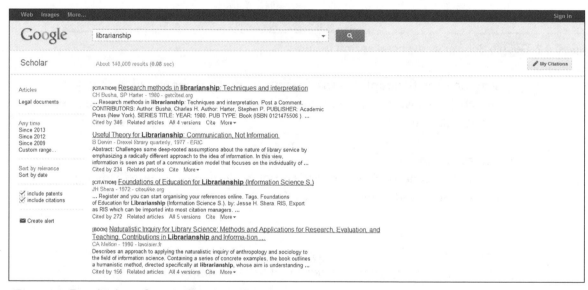

Figure 8.3 Results for a Google Scholar article search of *librarianship*

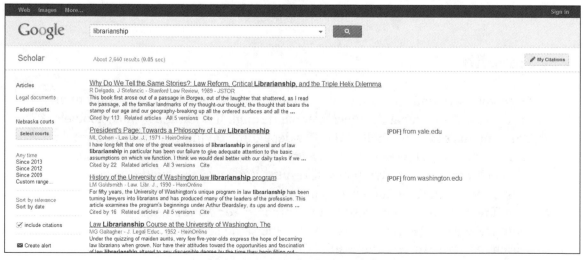

Figure 8.4 Results for a Google Scholar legal document search of *librarianship*

hyperlink goes only to a citation (and abstract if available) and not the article itself.
Links off to the right.

- *Author(s)*
The names of all authors associated with the article or legal document as they are listed on the article (e.g. some may have a full name, while others may have just a first initial and a last name).

- *Publication and publication year*
The year in which the article or legal document was published is almost always included. When available, the year is preceded by the name of the original journal in which the article or legal document was published.

- *Source*
The source is the domain name or publication name for the version of the article or legal document being linked to. In the case that Google may have additional sources for the result, those can be found via the Other Versions link, described below.

- *Snippet*
A brief excerpt of the article or legal document appears, typically three lines long, with the search keyword(s) highlighted.

- *Cited by*
Here you will see the number of other articles or legal documents that Google Scholar is aware of that cite this result. Clicking on this hyperlink will display a new page of results listing the articles that cite the initial result (figure 8.5).

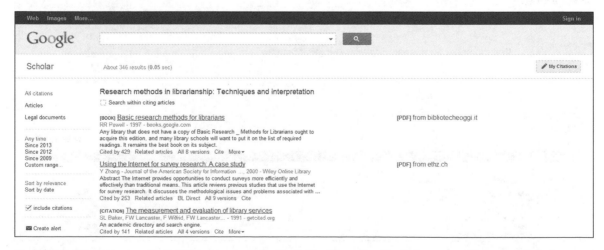

Figure 8.5 Cited by results for "Research methods in librarianship: Techniques and interpretation"

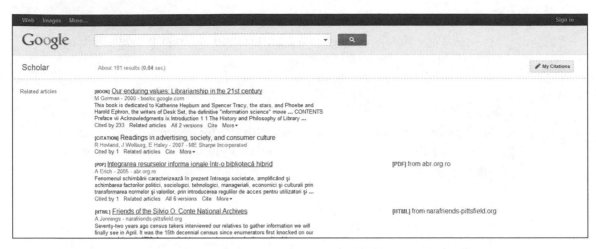

Figure 8.6 Related articles for "Our enduring values: Librarianship in the 21st century"

- *Related Articles*
  Clicking this link presents you with a new page of results of articles related to the topic on the initial result (figure 8.6).

- *Cached version (this link does not appear for Legal Document results)*
  If Google has a cached version of the article, clicking this link will display that version. This is useful for instances when the hyperlink on the title no longer works or is no longer available.

- *Library Search (this link does not appear for Legal Document results)*
  Clicking this link will perform a WorldCat.org search for the article in question (figure 8.7).

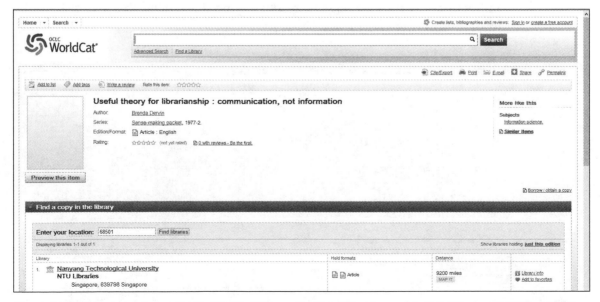

Figure 8.7 Library search results for "Useful theory for librarianship : communication, not information"

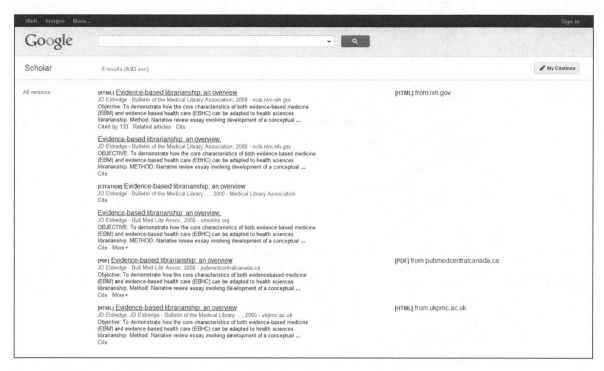

Figure 8.8 All versions for "Evidence-based librarianship: an overview"

- *Versions*

  In many cases, article or legal documents may be published in multiple locations or be presented online in multiple versions such as an HTML page, a PDF, and a citation. To see all the versions that Google has indexed of a particular result, click this link (figure 8.8).

There are also three gray buttons that you may find above and to the right of the search results. They are "My Citations," "Create an e-mail alert," and "Settings." We cover each of these to varying degrees at the end of this chapter.

SCHOLAR TOOLBELT

As we mentioned earlier in this chapter, the Scholar toolbelt is where you find the main differences between article searches and legal document searches. In this section we take on each one of these separately.

Articles Toolbelt

When you do an article search in Google Scholar, the results page will present you with what is probably the smallest of all the Google toolbelts. Here you only have a few options to choose from:

- *Search type*

  Here you can switch your search results from Articles to Legal Documents without having to re-enter your search terms.

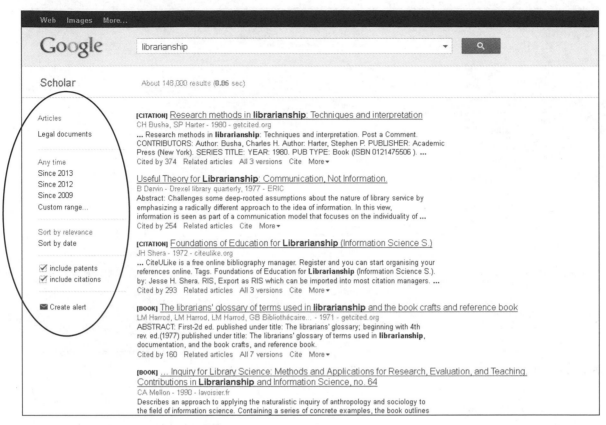

Figure 8.9 The Scholar Articles toolbelt

- *Time frame*
  Here you have five options: Any time (default), Since 2013, Since 2012, Since 2009, and Custom range . . . When it comes to the pre-listed years, come 2014 each of those years will increment accordingly. Clicking "Custom range . . ." will display two additional fields allowing you to specify a start and/or end year to limit your results (figure 8.9).

- *Include*
  Here you can check or uncheck, as appropriate, the inclusion of patents or citations in your search results.

Legal Documents Toolbelt

When it comes to your toolbelt options for Legal Documents, the list is just as short but no less useful (figure 8.10).

- *Search type*
  Here you can switch your search results from Legal Documents to Articles without having to re-enter your search terms.

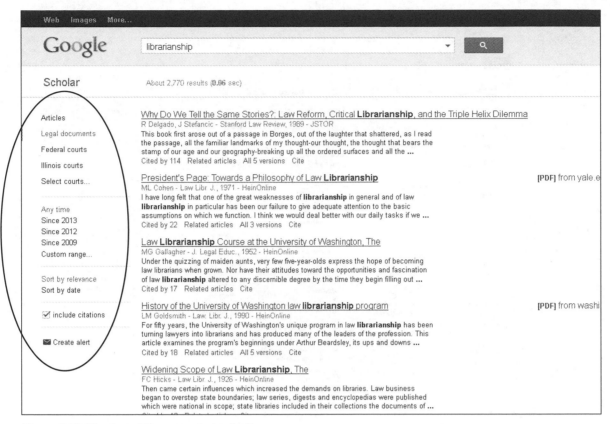

Figure 8.10 **The Legal Documents toolbelt**

- *Courts*

    By default, here you'll have the option to limit results to the Federal courts and the State court for which Google believe is currently relevant to you. Since we're in Nebraska, we're shown a limiter for Nebraska courts. Below that is a "Select courts" button, which when clicked will take you to the court selection page shown in figure 8.11. Here you can check or uncheck, as needed, which court's documents you wish to have appear in your results. If you need to uncheck whole groups, be aware of the "Select all" and "Clear selections" at the top of the page. Also, try unchecking one of the options for a state and watch what happens to the checkboxes for the individual courts within that state. When you're finished, click the "Done" button to return to your results. Clicking "Cancel" will return you to your results without applying any court selection changes.

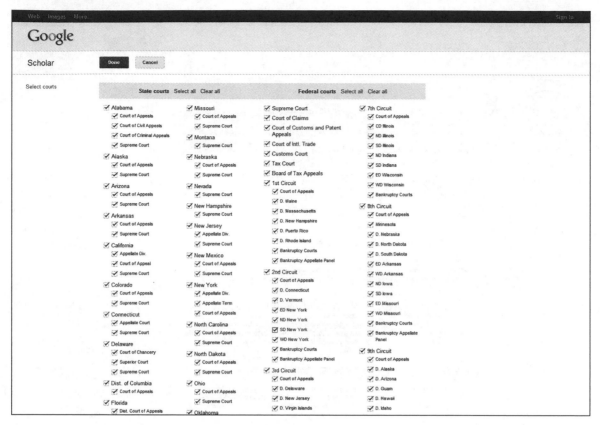

Figure 8.11 The Court Selection page

- *Time frame*
  Here you have five options: Any time (default), Since 2012, Since 2011, Since 2008, and Custom range . . . When it comes to the pre-listed years, we assume that come 2013 each of those years will increment accordingly. Clicking "Custom range . . ." will display two additional fields, allowing you to specify a start and/or end year to limit your results.

- *Include citations*
  Here you can check or uncheck this option, as appropriate, to show or not show citation results.

Additional Google Scholar Features

Lastly, there are a few additional links at the top of the Google Scholar home page (highlighted in figure 8.12) that need to be discussed. They are My Citations, Metrics, Alerts, and Settings.

Figure 8.12 Google Scholar links

MY CITATIONS

As we mentioned at the beginning of this chapter, the My Citations feature of Google Scholar allows authors of content that is searched by Google Scholar to track that content. However, since this feature is a bit beyond the scope of this book, we won't be covering this feature any further other than to include an example as figure 8.13.

Figure 8.13 My Citation for Michael P. Sauers

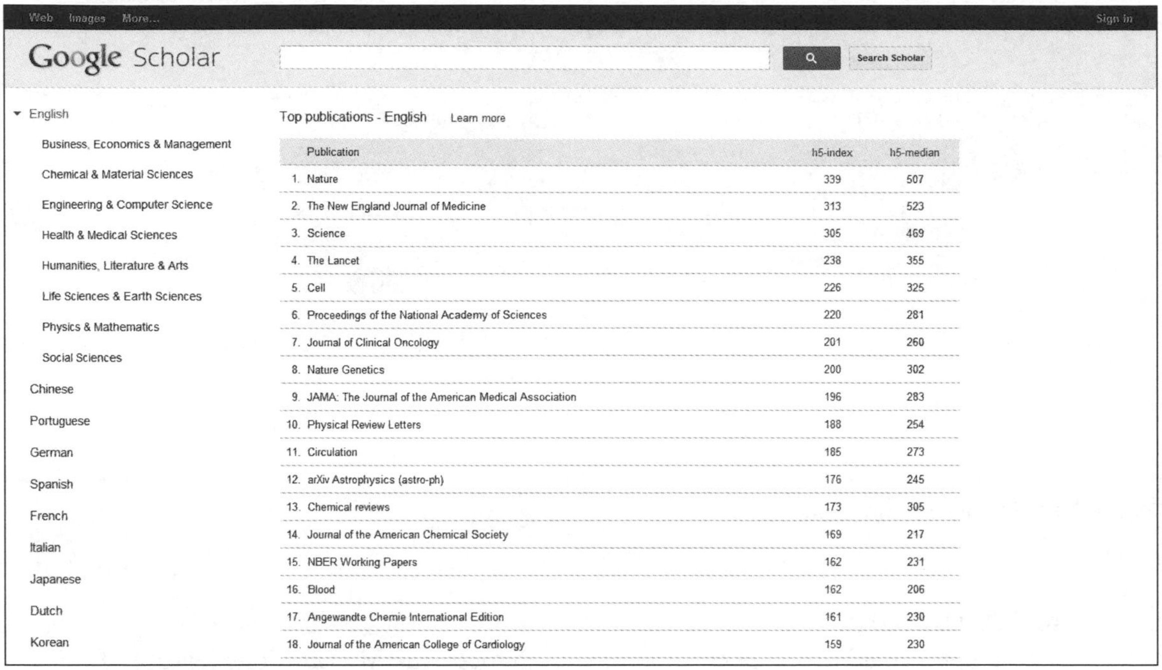

Figure 8.14 Example of Scholar Metrics for English titles

METRICS

To best describe what Scholar Metrics is (figure 8.14), we're going to quote Google's description of this service.

> Google Scholar Metrics provide an easy way for authors to quickly gauge the visibility and influence of recent articles in scholarly publications. While most researchers are familiar with the well-established journals in their field, that is often not the case with newer publications or publications in related fields—there're simply too many of them to keep track of! Scholar Metrics summarize recent citations to many publications, to help authors as they consider where to publish their new research.
>
> To get started, you can browse the top 100 publications in several languages, ordered by their five-year h-index and h-median metrics. You can also search for publications by their titles, and then compare the publications that are of interest to you. Finally, if you wish to see which articles in a publication were cited the most and who cited them, click on its h-index number to view the articles as well as the citations underlying the metrics.

For more details on just what is included in Scholar Metrics and how they're calculated, please refer to the Scholar Metrics help page via the "Learn more" link at the top of the page.

ALERTS

Via both this link on the Google Scholar home page and "Create an e-mail alert" links on search results pages, you can quickly and easily create searches for which you are automatically notified of new results. Taking advantage of this feature allows you to set up a search you would normally do on a regular basis and then just sit back and wait for the new results to be sent to you. Figure 8.15 shows the Scholar Alerts page with one alert already set up. (Logging in to a Google account is required for Alerts to work.)

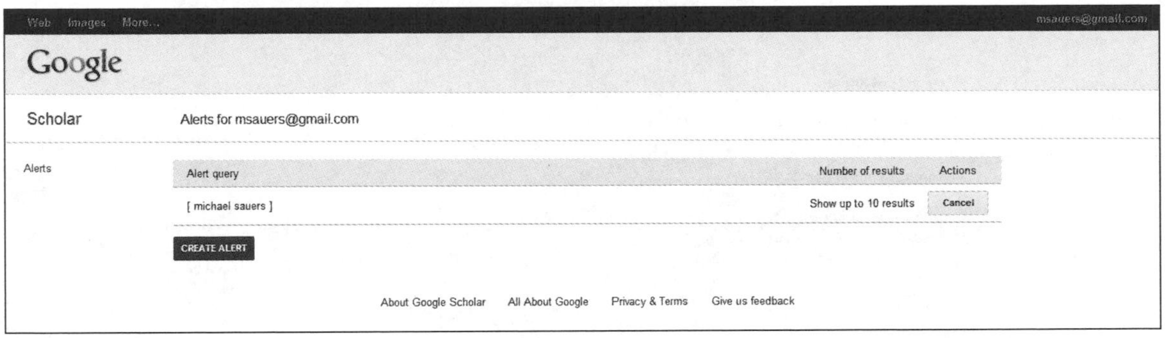

Figure 8.15 The Scholar Alerts page with one alert

The version of alerts that are created here are similar to, and somewhat less customizable, than those available via the full Google Alerts system that we cover in chapter 11. Therefore we'll leave the coverage of additional details for that chapter.

SETTINGS

Google Scholar's settings are broken down into three sections/screens. They are "Search results," "Languages," and "Library links." Let's take a look at what's available in each one.

Search Results

In this section you can control what you're searching and how those results are displayed (figure 8.16). The options are:

- *Collections*
  These are the same options that are available beneath the search box on the Google Scholar home page. By changing your options regarding search articles, patents, and legal documents, you change the default setting on the search home page.

- *Results per page*
  Here you can change the number of search results retuned per page to 10 (default), 20, 30, 50 or 100. Please note that Google does state "Google's default (10 results) provides the fastest results."

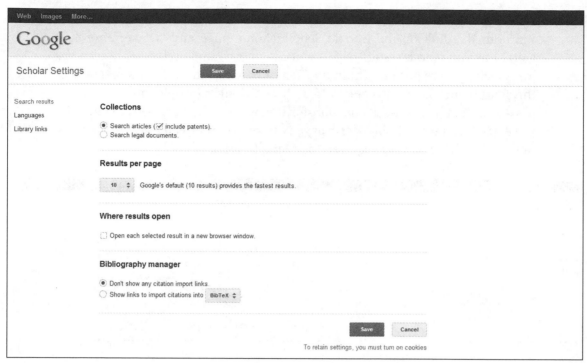

Figure 8.16 Google Scholar search results settings

- *Where results open*
  By default, clicking on a search result opens the article or document in the same window. Checking this option causes articles and documents to be opened in a new window instead. However, depending on your browser settings, links may open in a new tab instead of a new window.

- *Bibliography manager*
  There's a good chance that those doing regular scholarly research are using some sort of citation management software for organizing their research. If you're one of those individuals, this feature is for you. By default, Google Scholar does not provide links for automatically down-loading citations into citation management software; however, here you can choose the "Show links to import citations into" option and then choose BibTeX, EndNote, RefMan, or RefWorks (the four supported programs at the time of this writing). Once you've done this, you'll see an additional link at the end of each search result (figure 8.17) that, when clicked, will initiate an import of that citation into your selected program.

Languages

In this section you control the language options of Google Scholar (figure 8.18). They are:

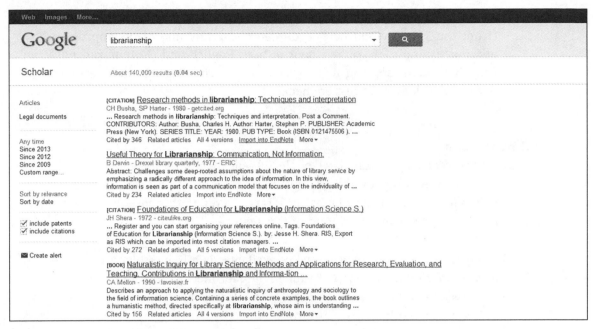

Figure 8.17 Google Scholar search results with EndNote import links

- *For Google text*

  This setting allows you to choose from forty different languages for displaying Google "tips and messages." In other words, here you are changing the language used by Google to display Google Scholar's interface. This does not affect the search results. That's the next setting.

- *For search results*

  By default, Google Scholar searches for content in any language. However, if you are looking for results in one or more specific languages

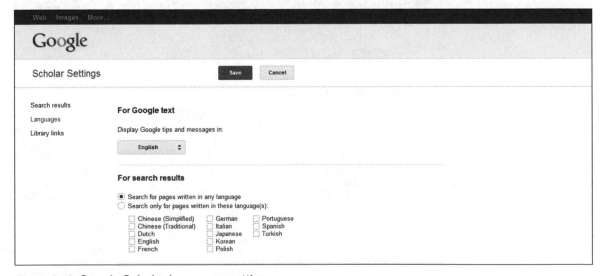

Figure 8.18 Google Scholar languages settings

(from the 13 provided here), you can check any and all as appropriate. For example, if you're fluent in both English and German but not French or Chinese, you may wish to check the English and German options and leave the rest unchecked.

Library Links

Lastly, in this section you can give Google Scholar the ability to search World-Cat, as we've previously described, but also the contents of other libraries that participate in the "Library Links" program. Again, in this case it is best to quote from Google's own description of this feature.

> For libraries that make their resources available via a link resolver, we are now offering the option to include a link for their patrons to these resources as a part of the Google Scholar search results.
>
> How does it work?
>
> On-campus users at participating schools will see additional links in Google Scholar search results which facilitate access to their library's resources. These links lead to the library's servers which, in turn, direct them to the full-text of the article.

Since we can't assume that most of our readers are at one of the participating libraries or have the skills to set up a link resolver as needed to allow their library to participate, we'll not be going into any additional detail about this feature here. However, we have included figures 8.19 through 8.21 to give you an idea of the options available.

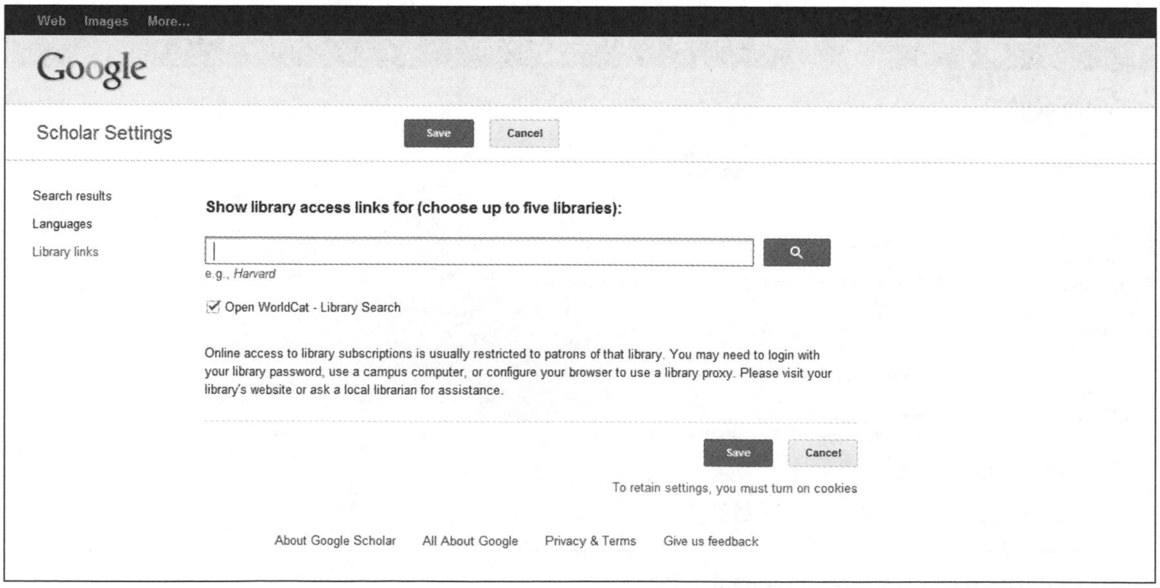

Figure 8.19 Google Scholar library links settings (default)

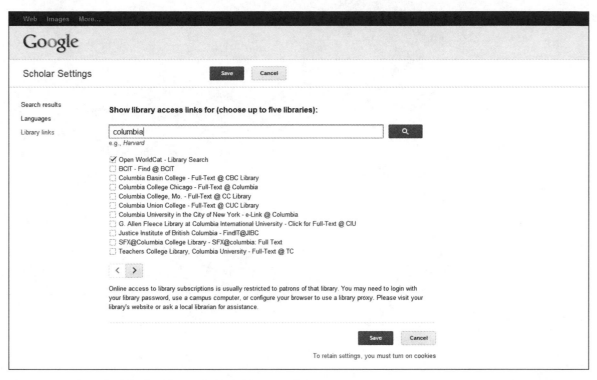

Figure 8.20 Google Scholar library links search results

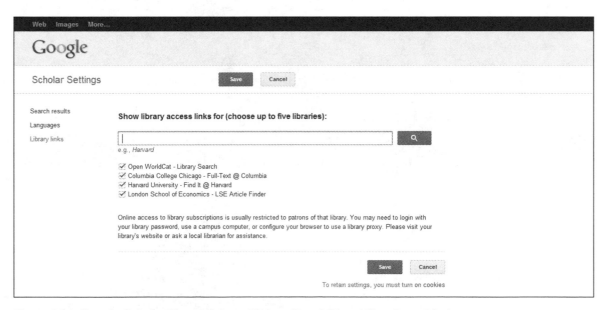

Figure 8.21 Google Scholar library links settings with additional libraries added

One last note: on each of the setting screens there is a "Save" button. Be sure to save your preferences before you leave the screen or else they will not keep. Also, Google Scholar settings rely on cookies being enabled in your browser in order for your settings to be stored. So, if you find that setting changes are not being kept, check your browser's cookie settings.

chapter 9

Google Patents

ACCORDING TO DICTIONARY.COM, a patent is "the exclusive right granted by a government to an inventor to manufacture, use, or sell an invention for a certain number of years." Since it is a right granted by the government, all records relating to patent applications and issuances are a matter of public record. The US Patent and Trademark office does offer a way to search these documents (http://www.uspto.gov/patents/process/search), but to many it is considered much harder to use and offers fewer options for searching when compared to the patent search system offered by Google.

Before we get into how to search patents via Google, both of us feel that we must stress to you that we have discovered that patent research is a very specific skill that takes a lot of experience to master—experience that neither of us have. As a result we'd like to point out that that the skills you'll learn from this chapter are designed for librarians that do not need to do this on a regular basis or are just looking for some basic information. If you have a patron looking for someone to do extensive patent research in preparation for a patent filing, we highly suggest you point them in the direction of a professional such as a patent attorney.

Basic Search

Google's patent search can be accessed by going to http://www.google.com/patents. As with most other Google search interfaces, you'll be presented with the basic search interface as shown in figure 9.1. Enter your keywords and

Figure 9.1 Basic patent search

choose either the "Google Search" or "I'm Feeling Lucky" buttons described in chapter 1.

Advanced Search

Unfortunately, there is no link to the advanced patent search on the basic search screen. However, there are two ways to still access it. The first is to perform a basic search and on the results page, scroll to the bottom and click the "Advanced Search" link there. If you do it this way, you will be presented with the advanced patent search interface with the keywords from your basic search already filled in.

The other option is to enter the URL directly: http://www.google.com/advanced_patent_search. If you access it this way, you'll be provided with blank search fields as shown in figure 9.2.

Figure 9.2 The Advanced Patent Search page

At the top of the advanced search form you will see the standard set of "Find results" options, all of which have been previously described in detail in chapter 1.

- With all of the words
- With the exact phrase
- With at least one of the words
- Without the words
- Results per page

After the standard options, you'll be presented with the patent specific options. They are:

- *Patent number*
  If you have a specific patent number you wish to find, enter it here. Example: *D483817*

- *Title*
  If you know the specific title of a patent, or you just wish to search for patents in which a certain keyword appears in the title, enter it here. Example: *techniques for displaying emails listed in an email inbox*

- *Inventor*
  If you are searching for patents by a certain individual you may enter it here. You may include the first name, last name, or both. Example: *linus torvalds*

- *Original assignee*
  Patents created by one person or group of people may be assigned to another, such as their employer for example. To find patents that were originally assigned to an individual or company, enter that name here. You may include the first name, last name, or both. Example: *microsoft*

- *Current U.S. classification*
  US patents are each classified under one or more categories for organizational purposes. The number of classifications are too many to be listed here. A full list can be found at http://www.uspto.gov/web/patents/classification/uspcindex/indextouspc.htm. To search for patents in one or more classifications, enter a comma delimited list in this field. Example: *562*

- *International classification*

  Similar to the US classification system, there is also an international classification system. To search for patents in one or more classifications, enter a comma delimited list in this field. Example: *5*

- *Patent type/status*

  When it comes to patent type, most US patents are "Utility" patents. Patents of other types, such as design and plant patents, have letters designating their type preceding their patent numbers. More details on patent types can be found at http://www.uspto.gov/patft/help/contents.htm. Because Google infers the patent type from the grant number, they only search granted patents when you specify a type. For status, Google indexes both patent applications and granted patents. Here you have the option to limit your search to the following types and statuses: Any type/status (default), Applications, Issued patents, Utility, Design (DD), Plant (P), Defensive publication (T), Additional Improvements (AI), and Statutory invention registration (H).

- *Date*

  Here you may restrict your results to patents from anytime (default), or a date range specified by year and month.

- *Restrict date by*

  If you do limit your results by date, you should then specify whether you wish that date to indicate the filing date of the patent (default) or the issue date.

As with the other Google search interfaces, each of the above-listed limiting fields have a matching "command line" search that you can use to initiate such a search from the search box. For example, entering *D483817* into the patent number field is the same as typing *patent:D483817* into the search box. The best way to find all the command-line options is to perform some sample advanced searches and note what appears in the search box on the results screen.

Results

In order to demonstrate the results of a patent search and to show you the items available in the patent search results options and tools, we'll be using a very simple yet broad search that gives us a good number of interesting results to manipulate. Figure 9.3 shows a result for a patent search on *telephone.*

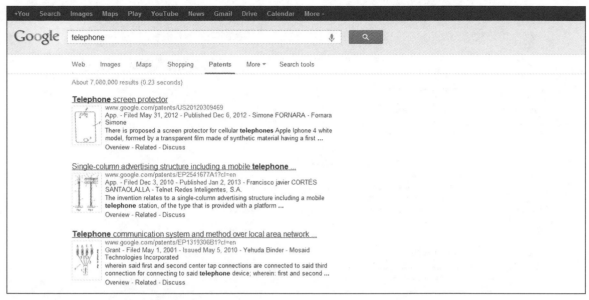

Figure 9.3 Patent search results for *telephone*

RESULTS PRESENTATION

For each result presented you'll be shown the following information:

- The title of the patent, which is a hyperlink to the "About This Patent" page
- An associated image of the first page of the patent, which is also hyperlinked to the "About This Patent" page
- The URL of the full record.
- The US Patent Number
- Filing date and/or issuing date as appropriate
- The assignee name
- A "patent snippet" to give some context to the result
- Links to the patent's Overview, a Related link to the Prior Art Finder, and a Discuss link to the Ask Patents website (these links will be discussed later in this chapter)

ABOUT THIS PATENT

As interesting as patent number 296829, issued in 1884, may be, we're going to go ahead and look at the About This Patent page for patent number D278433 from 1982, as this patent has more information available and is therefore a better example to work with.

To get to the About This Patent page, click on either the image or title of the patent on the results page. This will bring up the page shown in figure 9.4, which shows the patent overview.

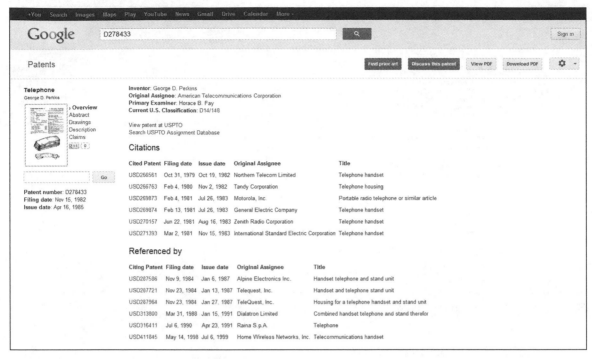

Figure 9.4 About This Patent for US Patent D278433

As with most other Google pages, you'll first have the black Google toolbar across the top of the screen, followed by the gray search bar. Below that you're reminded that you are currently working with "Patents" off to the left, and off to the right you'll see buttons to "Find prior art," "Discuss this patent." "View PDF" and "Download PDF." Lastly the gear icon will give you access to the Advanced Patent Search and your Web History if you're logged into Google.

Another important feature of this page is the search box on the left. Entering keywords here allows you to perform a search of the text of this patent. For example, figure 9.5 shows the results of searching for the word *xmas* within this patent. Again, notice that the display of these results is similar to that in Google Books.

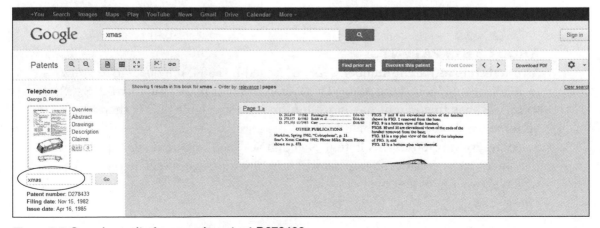

Figure 9.5 Search results for *xmas* in patent D278433

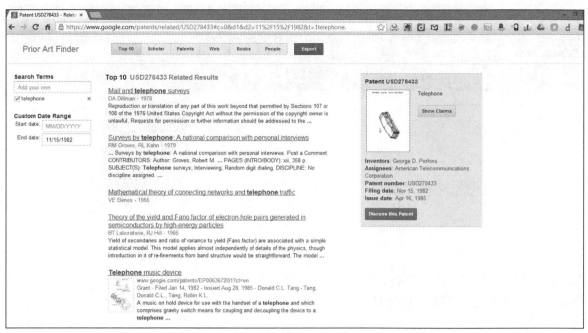

Figure 9.6 Prior Art Finder for US Patent D278433

Prior Art Finder

Patents are typically granted only if the invention is new, meaning no one else has come up with the same idea and patented it themselves. To prove this, applicants must search previous patents and include the results in their own patent application. With the Prior Art Finder, Google has made this much easier for applicants and researchers.

When you click the "Find prior art" button, Google pulls terms from the patent document you are viewing and automatically runs a new search (figure 9.6). The results are pulled from Google Patents, Google Scholar, Google Books, and the web in general. It defaults to showing you the Top 10 results, but you can choose to limit the list to results from each of the sources, using the buttons above the results. From the "People" button, you can search by inventor. Using the green "Export" button, the results can also be exported to a spreadsheet file.

On the left side of the screen, there is an additional search box to add more terms to narrow your prior art results. In the Custom Date Range field, the end date automatically defaults to the date of the original patent filing. You can change this if you like and add a Start date. On the right is basic information about the original patent, with a link back to it and a button to "Discuss this patent," which is explained in the next section of this chapter.

Ask Patents Website

Clicking the "Discuss this patent" button will bring you to the Ask Patents website. Ask Patents is part of the Stack Exchange group of question-and-

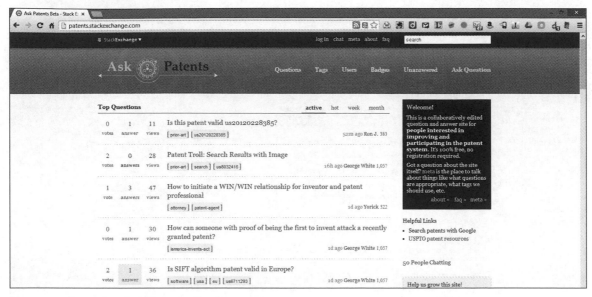

Figure 9.7 Browsing Ask Patent questions

answer sites. These are sites on specific topics where one can publicly ask questions and other people can answer them. Through this collaborative process, Ask Patents is attempting to create databases of information that people really want and need. You can ask a question about this patent or see what questions others have asked. It's a good place to learn more about the patent process and how others are using it (figure 9.7).

Read the Patent

Clicking "View PDF" will open a PDF with the complete text of the patent displayed. Figure 9.8 shows the PDF view screen for US Patent D278433.

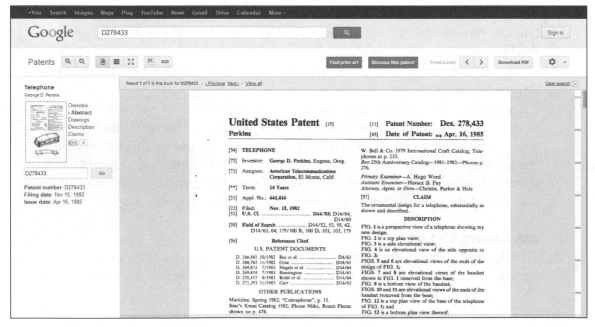

Figure 9.8 Reading Patent D278433

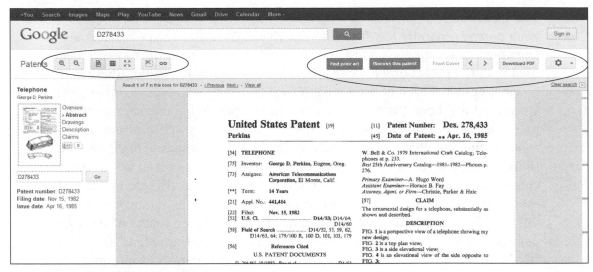

Figure 9.9 Viewing the patent PDF

While viewing the PDF, above the document you'll find buttons to zoom in and out, view single or multiple pages, view full screen, search the document, Download the original, add to Google Drive or Print the PDF (figure 9.9).

Download PDF

For easy saving, printing, and offline reading, click the "Download PDF" button to download a PDF file of the patent. Figure 9.10 shows a patent's PDF file displayed in a PDF reading program.

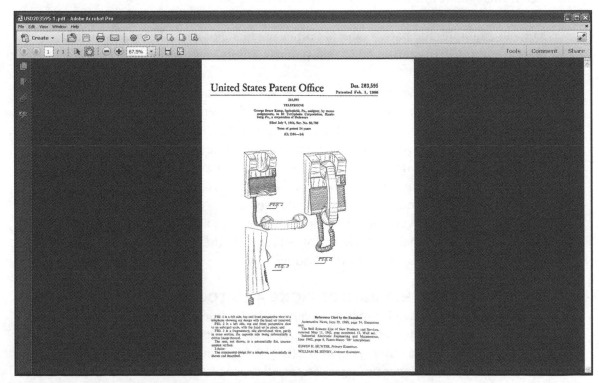

Figure 9.10 The PDF of patent D203595 in a PDF reader

Patent Views

Each patent generally has five different views: Overview (default), Abstract, Drawings, Descriptions, and Claims. Each of these are parts of the document filed with the patent office. Depending on the length of the patent, there may be more or less of each of these areas. Clicking on any of the views (other than Overview) will open the patent in a new frame, presenting that section of the patent at the top of the screen. Above the document you'll find buttons to zoom in and out, view single or multiple pages, view full screen, highlight and share a clip, and get a URL for this patent to share with others. Because our current example is a patent of only a few pages in length, clicking on each of these options will not present substantially different results. Along with these links on the left are the title and author of the patent, an image of the first page of the patent, a Google+ button, a "Search within this patent" field and "Go" button, the patent number, filing date, and issue date (as appropriate).

Patent Overview

The majority of this page contains an overview of the patent as a whole. Here you will find the name(s) of the inventor(s), the original assignee, the name of the primary examiner, and the current US classification(s) of the patent—each of which include hyperlinks to searches for those names and numbers in their relevant fields. Also, not all of this information may appear on each patent overview. If the information is not available, it will not be displayed.

Next you'll find links to "View patent at USPTO," website to see the information at the patent office and to "Search USPTO Assignment Database" to see if this patent has been assigned to someone else.

Below this you'll find both citations and references as available. In our current example, the patent cites six other patents. For each there is the Cited Patent's number (hyperlinked to that patent), Filing Date, Issue Date, Original Assignee, and Title.

Similarly, nine other patents reference this patent and are listed next with the same information and hyperlinks as the cited patents.

If there are no other patents that either cite or are cited by the current patent, no information will appear in the patent's overview.

Next you're presented with the Claims of the patent. Typically these are very brief but in some cases can be much longer. If you're looking for a brief summary of the patent, this is the place to look.

Lastly, thumbnail versions of any and all drawings associated with the patent are displayed. Each of these is hyperlinked to the matching page in the patent and will be displayed in the reading view.

PATENT SEARCH RESULTS OPTIONS AND TOOLS

As with all Google search types, you can further refine your search using the filtering options in the panel above your search results.. If you would like to expand your search to other types of content besides Patents, you can switch to see results such as Images or News. To see all types of content, choose "Web."

Click "Search tools" for the patent-specific filters. The following pull-down menus will appear below the content options:

- *Which date*

  Here you can choose to show results from "Any date" (default), "Restrict by filing date" or "Restrict by publication date." These options make the most sense if you have previously limited your search results by date via the advanced search and now wish to change those results.

- *Patent office*

  Google offers results from "Any Patent Office," date (default), the United States Patent and Trademark Office, or the European Patent Office.

- *Filing status*

  By default you will receive results in the category of "Any filing status," meaning you can see patents that are both applications and issued patents. Here you can choose to limit your results to just "Applications" or "Issued patents."

- *Patent type*

  As previously discussed in the advanced search section, patents come in different types. Here you can limit your results to Any patent type (default), Utility, Design, Plant, Defensive Publication, Additional Improvement, or Statutory Invention Registration.

- *Sort*

  You can choose to re-sort your results by relevance (default), filing date: latest, or filing date: oldest. Figures 9.11 and 9.12 show our *telephone* search results sorted by latest and oldest respectively.

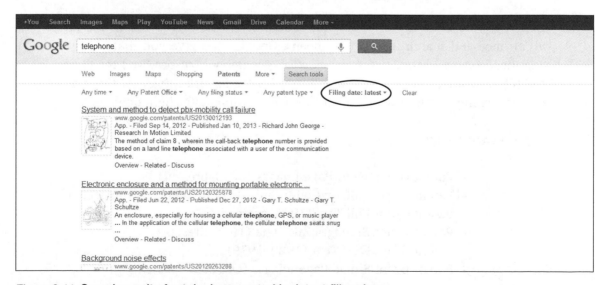

Figure 9.11 Search results for *telephone* sorted by latest filing date

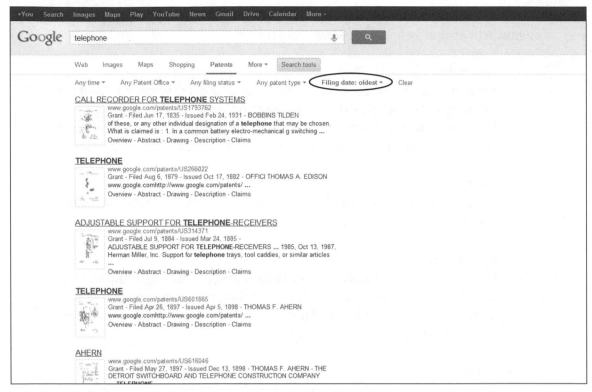

Figure 9.12 Search results for *telephone* sorted by oldest filing date

Finally you can choose to "Clear," which returns all limits and sorts back to their default settings and redisplays your results.

USPTO Bulk Downloads

Lastly, if you're someone looking for the ability to download the whole lot all at once and search it via other means, Google does give you that ability. Just head over to http://www.google.com/googlebooks/uspto.html for links to bulk downloads of both US Patents and US Trademark filings. At the time of this writing, the following patent files were available for bulk download:

- *Patent Grants*

    - Patent Grant Multi-Page Images (1790–present)
    - Patent Grant Full Text with Embedded Images (2001–present)
    - Patent Grant Full Text (1976–present)
    - Patent Grant Bibliographic Data (1976–present)
    - Patent Grant OCR Text (1920–1979)
    - Patent Grant Single-Page Images (Oct 2010–present)

- *Patent Application Publications*

  - PAIR (Patent Application Information Retrieval) Data
  - Patent Application Publication Multi-Page Images (2001–present)
  - Patent Application Publication Full Text with Embedded Images (2001–present)
  - Patent Application Publication Full Text (2001–present)
  - Patent Application Publication Bibliographic Data (2001–present)
  - Patent Application Single-Page Images (Oct 2010–present)

- *Additional Patent Data*

  - Patent Assignment Text (1980–present)
  - Patent Maintenance Fee Events (1981–present)
  - Patent Classification Information (current)
  - Patent IFW Petition Decisions

chapter 10

Google Books

USING WEB-BASED TOOLS to search for print materials is now considered commonplace. However, when it comes to searching for content *within* print material, many of us are still not all that comfortable. Granted, librarians constantly use online databases that contain digital versions of existing print content, but this isn't exactly what we mean.

What we're talking about is the ability to do full-text searches of traditionally print-only books, to find particular words or phrases within a book, so that once you've confirmed that the book has what you're looking for, you can find the physical book in your collection or from another source. Think of it as an online full-text index that goes well beyond the one found in the back of the book itself. This is the essence of Google Books.

Google is currently indexing books that are both in the public domain and copyrighted works. Ian-copyright works are sourced both from publishers from whom Google has permission—Google's Partner Program (https://Books.google.com/partner) and from the collections of nearly 20 libraries around the world, Google's Library Project (http://books.google.com/googlebooks/partners.html). Books may be searched for from within the standard simple Google search interface. You can also browse for books by subject and genre via the Google Book Search home page at http://books.google.com (see figure 10.1). As in the rest of this book, we focus on searching as opposed to browsing.

Figure 10.1 The Google Books home page

BASIC SEARCH

The book search is located on the Google Books Search home page, as shown in figure 10.1, under "Researching a topic?" In this case, just type in the keyword(s) you're searching for (title, author, subject, etc.) and click the "Search Books" button. This interface supports all the same functionality as the search box for Google's web search, as described in chapter 2.

ADVANCED SEARCH

As with most other Google search services, there is an advanced search option. However, finding it is a bit difficult, as a link to it is presented to you only at the bottom of a results page. Otherwise you can access it directly via the URL http://books.google.com/advanced_book_search.

With the advanced book search interface (see figure 10.2) you will be presented with the following options for searching: find results (with four sub-options), search, language, title, author, publisher, subject, publication date, ISBN, and ISSN.

The "Find results" area allows you to build a Boolean-based query without knowing the specifics of Boolean operators.

- *With all the words*
  Any keywords entered into this field will be present in the search results (Boolean AND).

- *With the exact phrase*
  Multiple words entered into this field will be treated as a phrase (as if enclosed in quotation marks).

- *With at least one of the words*
  At least one of the words entered into this field must be present in the search results (Boolean OR).

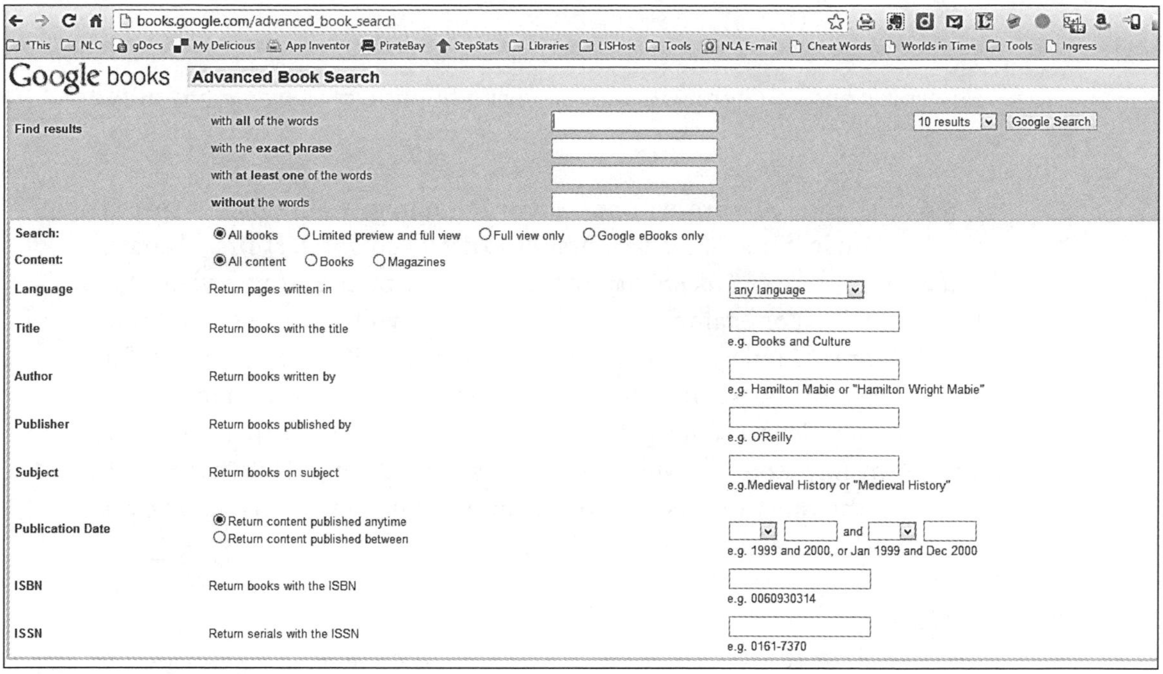

Figure 10.2 Advanced Book Search

- *Without the words*
  Results will not include any of the words entered into this field (Boolean NOT). Additionally, you can specify 10, 20, 30, 50, or 100 results per page in this area.

- *Search*
  You can specify whether you wish to search "all books" in the collection, only books with a "Limited preview and full view" or "Full view only" results display, or "Google eBooks only"—which actually performs a search of only books available for purchase (or completely available for free) from the commercial side of Google Books. We generally recommend that you keep your searches to all books to retrieve the most results.

- *Content*
  Here you can limit your search to "All content," "Books," or "Magazines."

- *Language*
  Google allows you to limit your results to one of more than 40 different languages, ranging from Arabic to Vietnamese. Of course, the number of results will vary; be sure to search for keywords in the appropriate language. Chances are, searching for English keywords within Arabic texts will not retrieve many results regardless of the size of the Arabic collection.

- *Title*

  Keywords entered here will appear within the title of the search results.

- *Author*

  Keywords entered here will appear in the author name of the search results. Single names (*koontz*), first last (*dean koontz*), last first (*koontz, dean*), and phrases (*"dean koontz"*) are all accepted but may yield different results. For example, a search for *koontz* will retrieve the authors Dean Koontz, Linda D. Koontz, and Louis Knott Koontz. Searches for *"dean koontz"* and *koontz, dean* will retrieve only Dean Koontz, while searches for *dean koontz* will retrieve Dean Koontz, Dean R. Koontz, and Dean Ray Koontz (who are all the same person). This last search retrieves the most results due to the different listings of his name over his publishing career.

- *Publisher*

  You can limit the search results by entering the name of a publisher in this field. We recommend using quotation marks on multiword publisher names (*"cemetery dance"* vs. *cemetery dance*) for a higher degree of accuracy.

- *Subject*

  This field searches the subject headings associated with each book. The source of these subjects is unspecified within the Google system, so we suggest you keep this type of search limited until you become more familiar with the results. This field can also be considered a genre search when searching for fiction.

- *Publication date*

  Here you can choose between "Return content published anytime" and "Return content published between." If you choose the latter you can then fill in either or both start and end date range information. Filling in both allows you to limit your results to books published within that inclusive date range. In other words, "Return books published between Jan 2005 and Dec 2007" will return results published in 2005, 2006, and 2007. It is also important to note that this is the publication date, not the copyright date; if a book was first published in 1969 but was reprinted in 2006, the previously described search will return it as a result.

- *ISBN*

  If you've got an ISBN and want to see if the book is in the system, just enter it here. Since ISBNs uniquely identify a particular edition of a title, you should receive only a single result.

- *ISSN*

  As with ISBN, you can specify an ISSN if you're searching for a periodical. We stick with books for the examples in this chapter.

Once you've filled in the appropriate fields, click the "Google Search" button to perform your search and retrieve the results.

BOOK SEARCH RESULTS

Say you're looking for some information about Alexander Hamilton. (We'll worry about what you're looking for specifically a little later.) Let's perform a simple search for *alexander hamilton* to see what results we find (see figure 10.3).

The Google Books search results page is arranged like most of the other search results pages. The search box, with your search terms included, is at the top, along with links related to Google accounts and Google + services. Just below this, the links to other types of searches are presented, followed by the Search tools link, which provides more search limiters. Next, you will find the number of results and the length of time it took Google to perform the search—and all the way to the right is the gear icon to access your general search settings, web history, and search help. If there are any Ads or Sponsored links, they will appear either at the top of your results and/or off to the right. At the bottom of the page are the standard next/previous page of results links and some suggested searches related to your search term(s).

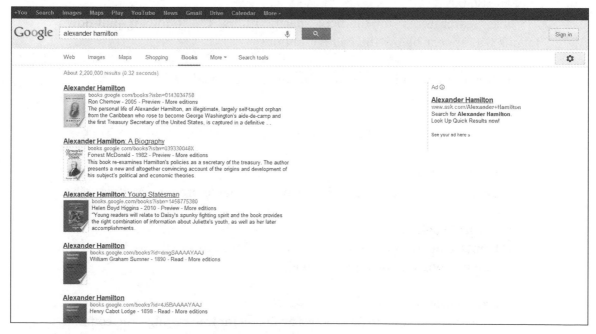

Figure 10.3 Results for an *alexander hamilton* search

Next we come to the individual search results themselves. In most cases, either the cover or first page of the book will be displayed to the left of the record. The text portion of the record will start with the title of the book. Clicking on either the image or the title will take you to either the preview of the book (if available) or the "About this book" page.

The next line contains the name of the author (hyperlinked for an author search), the publication year, number of pages, and preview link if available. This is then followed by a brief two- to three-line description or excerpt from the book. With newer books, this is typically taken from the dust jacket copy. Please note that not all of this information will be available for all records. The final line of a result provides us with a "More editions" link (if available), and an "Add to my library" link, which we discuss further later in this chapter.

The "More editions" link will take you to a page that presents you with other editions of the same title. For example, you might receive listings for hardcover and paperback editions of the same title. More historical items might provide you with listings for editions from many different publishers, containing not only the same basic text but also additional writings by the same author and/or forewords or afterwords by other authors.

THE BOOK SEARCH RESULTS OPTIONS AND TOOLS

As with most other Google search results screens, you have access to context-sensitive filtering options in the panel above your search results. If you would like to expand your search to other types of content besides Books, you can switch to see results such as Images or News. To see all types of content, choose "Web."

Click "Search tools" for the book-specific filters. The following pull-down menus will appear below the content options.

The first section limits the source of content returned.

- *Any books*
  This default option shows you all results.

- *Preview available*
  Limits your results to only books with available preview content.

- *Google eBooks*
  Limits your results to only content available through the commercial side of Google Books (pay or free).

- *Free Google eBooks*
  Limits your results to only books available for free through the commercial side of Google Books.

The next section limits the type of content returned.

- *Any document*
Returns both books and magazines (default).

- *Books*
Returns only books.

- *Magazines*
Returns only magazines.

The next section allows you to limit your results by date.

- *Any time*
Returns results from any time period (default).

- *21st century*
Returns only results from the 21st century.

- *20th century*
Returns only results from the 20th century.

- *19th century*
Returns only results from the 19th century.

- *Custom range . . .*
Allows you to enter a start and/or end date range for your results. As with this option in the advanced search, the dates given are inclusive. The one benefit of doing it here is that you can specify to the day, unlike only month and year in the advanced search interface (figure 10.4).

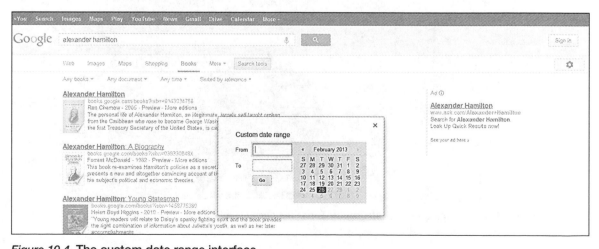

Figure 10.4 **The custom date range interface**

Lastly, you can choose from the following two sorting options:

- *Sorted by relevance*
  Displays results as determined by Google's relevancy ranking algorithm (default).

- *Sorted by date*
  Sorts the results by publication date in reverse chronological order (newest first).

BOOK CONTENT

Selecting a particular book will take you to the book's page. What information is provided here, and how much of the actual content of the book is shown, depends on such factors as the age of the book, the copyright status of the book, and the availability of the book for purchase through the commercial side of Google Books. For the rest of this chapter we use *Pops: A Life of Louis Armstrong* by Terry Teachout as our example (figure 10.5). This book is not available as full text but does have some preview content. It is also available for purchase through Google Books.

A lot of information is presented in this example, and with the web's hyperlinking technology, what you find here is just a starting point to much more. Let's take a moment to walk through all the information provided.

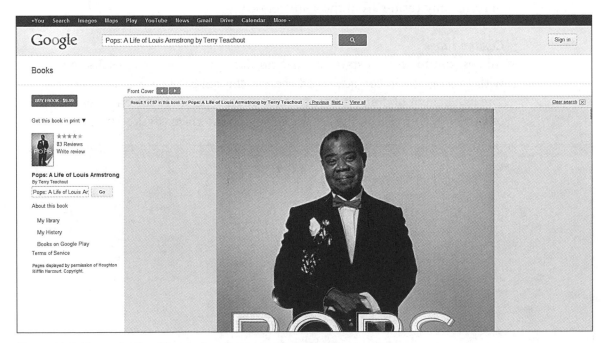

Figure 10.5 *Pops: A Life of Louis Armstrong* by Terry Teachout

Across the top of the page you'll see the standard black Google toolbar with the search bar just below it. Just above the book itself, you will find "Front Cover" with two blue arrow buttons. These buttons can be used to go to the next and previous available page in the book. The pages that are available are determined by the Preview version of the book, which is covered later in this chapter.

In the cream bar below that, you have < Previous and Next > links, which will bring you through the instances of your search term(s) in the book text. "View all" will bring up the parts of every page where your search term(s) appear. "Clear search X" will close the cream bar. Clicking on either of the blue arrow buttons will bring the cream bar back. To the left of the book you'll find (as available) a link to purchase the book electronically from Google Books, a link to "Get this book in print," which will link to various online bookstores and WorldCat to find the book in a library, a thumbnail of the cover along with a "Google+ +1" button, a five-star rating system, and links to online reviews and to write a review yourself.

Below this you'll find the title and the author of the current book and a search box that allows you to search the content of this book. You then have a series of links for "About this book," "My Library," "My History," and "Books on Google Play." Lastly you have a link to the Google Books Terms of Service, and copyright information about the book as it relates to Google Books.

Let's start by taking a look at the "About this book" page for our example (figure 10.6).

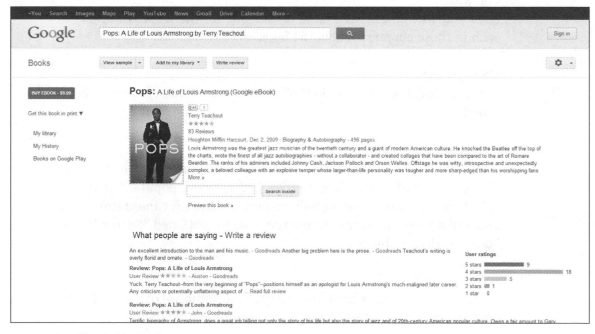

Figure 10.6 **About this book**

- *General information*
  Here you will find an image of the book's cover or first page, along with the title, author, publication year, publisher, subject (search hyperlinked), page count, and descriptive text. If the book has content available for review, a link to "Preview this book" appears beneath the description.

- *Search inside*
  At first this section of the page contains just a search box allowing you to search the contents of the book itself. We cover content searching in depth in the next section, but it is worth mentioning here solely for how it presents the results.

- *Reviews*
  This section presents titles, brief excerpts, sources, and links to online reviews of this book. Reviews from professional literature and major newspapers are weighted heavily here, but others are available with a little digging.

- *Related books*
  Google offers titles for books related to the topic of the book you're viewing. These of course are hyperlinked to their pages in Google Books.

- *Contents*
  Here you will find a basic table of contents for the book with links to each of those chapters within the book when available.

- *Other editions*
  This area lists the other editions of this book available via Google Book Search.

- *Common terms and phrases*
  This section lists hyperlinks of terms commonly used within the text. Think of this as if the book's index had a "most popular" category. Selecting any of these terms will perform a search for that term in the text and present the results in the previously mentioned "Search in this book" section of this page

- *About the author*
  This section presents a brief biography of the author(s) of the book. The date associated with this biography is also presented.

- *Bibliographic information*

    Google's bibliographical record for a book typically contains the title, author, edition, publisher, ISBN, length, and subjects (hyperlinked for easy cross-searching). Buttons for exporting these records in BiBTeX, EndNote, and RefMan formats are also made available.

PREVIEW THIS BOOK

As with the previous section, not all the items described here will be available with all books. Before we proceed, we want to explain the three different versions of availability that Google offers: full view, limited preview, and snippet view.

Full View

Full view means that the complete contents of the book are available for reading within Google Books Search (figure 10.7). This option is generally available only on books that are clearly out of copyright (pre-1923).

Limited Preview

Limited preview is generally available for books that have been contributed to Google Books Search through its publisher Partner Program. In this case,

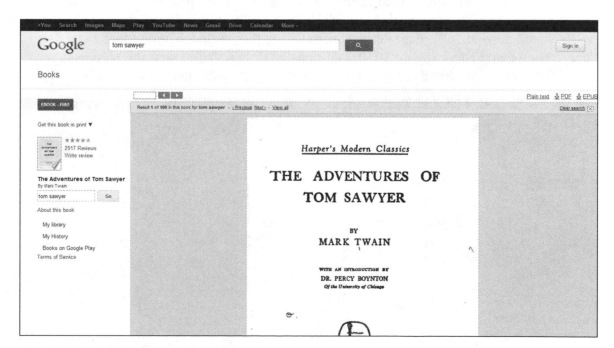

Figure 10.7 Full view

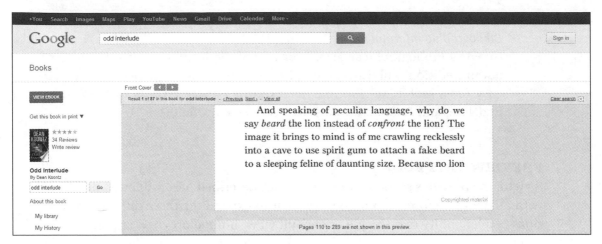

Figure 10.8 Limited preview

you're able to see a limited number of complete pages from the book. In some cases, these are specific pages or a certain number of pages of your choosing. The method and number are not determined by Google and therefore vary from book to book and publisher to publisher, so more specific information is unavailable. A limited preview page can be seen in figure 10.8.

Snippet View

The snippet view is generally reserved for books that are in-copyright but have been added to the collection via Google's Library Project and without the explicit permission of the copyright holder. The snippet view shows only small sections of a page of text surrounding the particular terms that have been searched for (figure 10.9). Additionally, the number of viewable snippets is limited, but that number is not explicitly stated by Google.

Figure 10.9 Snippet view

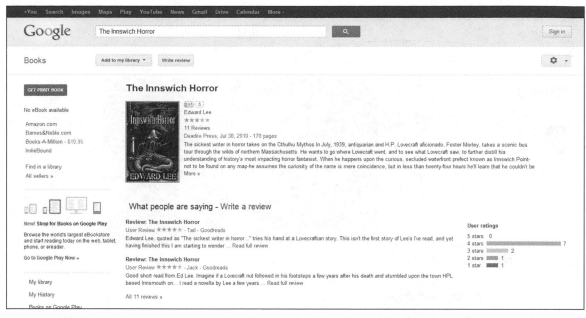

Figure 10.10 No preview

No Preview

In some cases, a book will have no content available online at all. Figure 10.10 shows an example of what you will be provided with in such a case.

When looking at a search results list, books will be labeled "Read this book," "Preview," "Snipped view," or "No preview" depending on the amount available. We use books with available previews for the rest of this section since our example book is not completely available. In all these views, any of your search keywords will be highlighted in yellow.

BOOK CONTENT NAVIGATION

To access the book navigation options, first choose "About this book" to the left of the book. Then choose "Preview this book" just below the general information about the book. Despite the amount of actual content available, the book's page will still generally show a good bit of detail about the boo, but the main focus is on the content of the book itself. So, in this section we focus on the buttons above the book's content and in the content windows itself.

Keeping in mind that the actual amount of a particular book will vary, let us now take you through the basic options of book navigation. Most of the navigation options are available in the bar near the top of the window, just above the book (figure 10.11). Here you'll find buttons for zooming, expanded view, linking/embedding, Add to my library, Write review, Contents, page forward, page back, and the Settings. We'll be focusing on the navigation-related buttons first and then mention the others. Additionally, you can navigate via scrolling and dragging. Let's take a look at each of these in a little more detail.

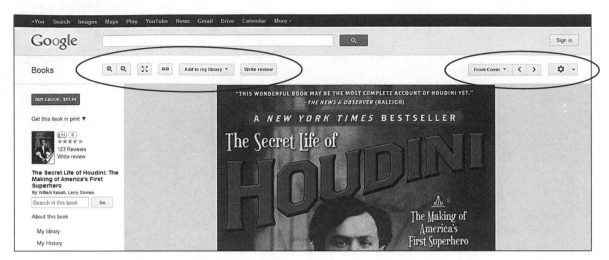

Figure 10.11 Navigation buttons

- *Scrolling and dragging*

  Located on the right of the screen is a scrollbar. By using this scrollbar, you can quickly scroll through the available contents of the book. Additionally, you can move your mouse pointer over the image to change it into a hand. Clicking and holding your left mouse button will "grab" the page and allow you to move the image up, down, left, or right with your mouse. This is especially handy when you're zoomed in on a page.

- *Zoom*

  The zoom buttons are located in the navigation bar, centered over the book image. Clicking on the minus magnifying glass icon will zoom out, while the plus magnifying glass icon will zoom in (figure 10.12).

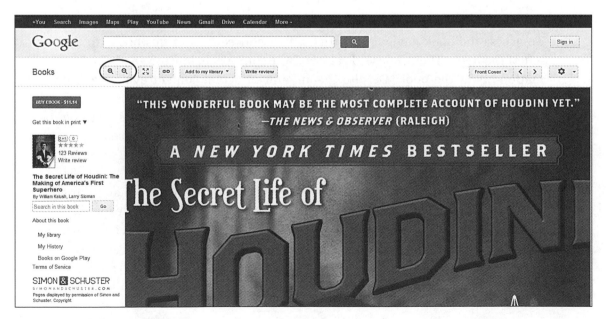

Figure 10.12 Full zoom example

Figure 10.13 Expanded view example

There are a total of five zoom levels.

- *Expanded view*
  The expanded view button removes most of the extraneous Google content from the screen and makes larger the view (single- or dual-page) that you are current viewing. Scrolling within the book continues to work or not based on the view you're in. To turn off expanded view, click the button again (figure 10.13).

- *Link/Embed*
  Clicking this button will open a small window containing the URL for linking directly to this book and the HTML necessary to embed this book into another web page. Copy the URL or HTML as needed and paste it into the appropriate location (figure 10.14).

Figure 10.14 The link/embed button

- *Add to my library*
  If you are logged into a Google account, hovering over this button will present you with "My Google eBooks" and (if available) a list of your previously created "shelves" in your personalized Google library. Otherwise, it will prompt you to log in to your Google account before you can proceed. Because this option is available only when you are logged into your Google account, it is not covered in this book.

- *Write review*
  If you are logged into a Google account, clicking this button takes you to another page into which you can enter and save your review of this book and provide your rating on a scale of one to five stars. If you are not logged in to a Google account, you will be prompted to log in before you can write a review. Since this option is available only when you are logged into your Google account, it is not covered in this book.

- *Contents (front cover)*
  This button will provide (if available) a list of locations within the book that when clicked will jump you to that location. Typically these are chapters, but not always. The locations available are dependent on the source material, and not all books may have this option (figure 10.15).

- *Previous/Next page*
  These icons are in the shape of left- and right-pointing triangles similar to the back and forward buttons in web browsers. Click the left-pointing triangle to go to the previous page and click the right-pointing triangle to go to the next page.

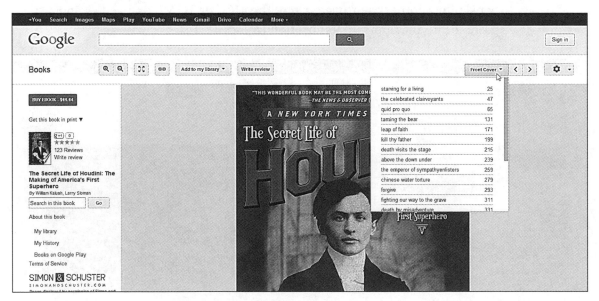

Figure 10.15 Table of contents example

Figure 10.16 The links under the gear icon

Now that we've covered the navigation buttons, there are just a few left to mention:

• Clicking "Settings" (the gear icon) provides you with links to My library, Help, Advanced Book Search (covered previously), and Web History (figure 10.16).

SEARCHING BOOK CONTENT

Searching for keywords within the text of a book is simple and can be done from any of the "Search in this book" fields previously mentioned. For simplicity's sake, let's use the one from the book's page.

Say you're previewing the book *Pops: A Life of Louis Armstrong* by Terry Teachout, interested in knowing about Louis Armstrong's thoughts on Miles Davis, and you believe that's something that would be covered in this book. So let's search in this book for *miles davis*. You're presented with 14 results in relevance order, as shown in figure 10.17. To switch the results to page order,

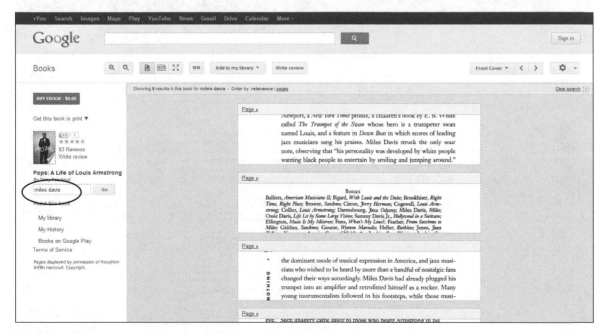

Figure 10.17 Search in the book results sorted by relevance

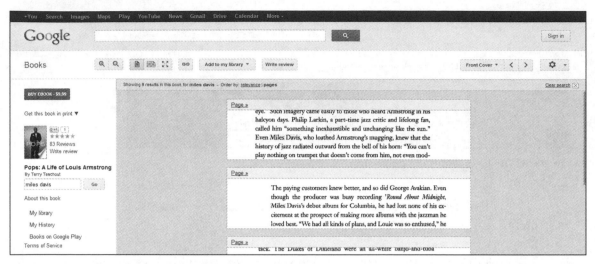

Figure 10.18 Search in the book results sorted by pages

click the "pages" link on the new cream-colored bar at the top of the content window (figure 10.18).

Each result presents a link (Page ») that takes you to the complete page (if available) and a brief contextual preview of that page's content. As you can see in figure 10.19, for some pages we're being told "No preview available for this page. Buy this book" because this book is available only under limited preview. To view a result in context, click on the page link. In figure 10.20, you can see that we've opened page 338, which talks about The Dukes of Dixieland band wishing folks like Dizzy Gillespie and Miles Davis had never been born.

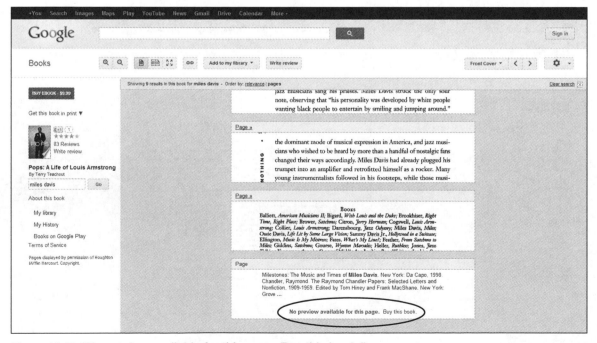

Figure 10.19 "No preview available for this page. Buy this book."

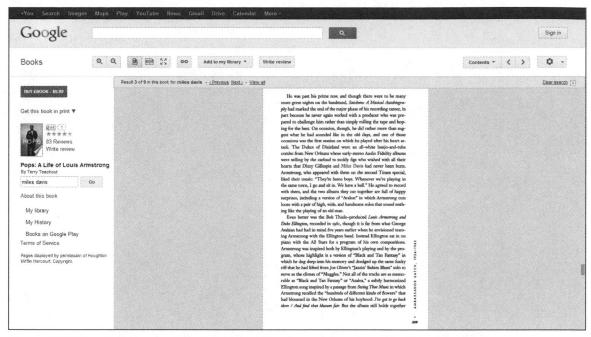

Figure 10.20 Preview of page 339 of *Pops: A Life of Louis Armstrong* by Terry Teachout

Moving to the next or previous result is done through the " < Previous" and "Next >" links in the cream-colored bar above the book's content. A "View all" link is also available to take you back to the results list. Lastly, off to the right is a "Clear search X" link, which will clear your results and return you to the book as you were prior to the search.

One last thing that you may not have noticed is that once you've searched within a book, you'll have two additional navigation buttons above the preview. These are for Single-page and Dual-page views of the content. All of our previous examples have been in single-page mode. Figure 10.21 shows an example of the dual-page mode.

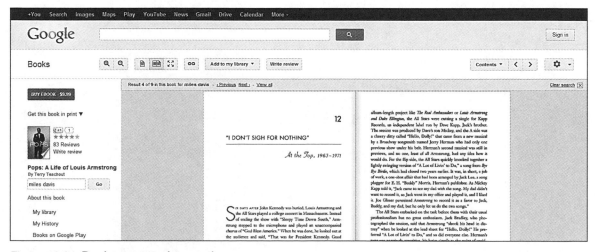

Figure 10.21 Dual-page preview mode

chapter 11

Google Alerts

NOW THAT WE'VE introduced you to and led you through all types of searches you can perform via Google, let's take a look at search from another angle. In most of our examples, we've looked at Google from the point of view of a reference situation, one in which every question you get is different from the last one. But what about when you have a question for which you'd like to receive regular updates of new results? Sure, you can schedule some time once a week to head on over to Google, type in your search query, get some results, and spend the time necessary to figure out which results are new and which you've seen before. But why not let Google do the work for you instead? This is where Google Alerts (http://www.google.com/alerts) can help you out.

Creating an Alert

Here's the scenario: Let's say you occasionally suffer from gout. There isn't any known cure for this type of arthritis, but there are many theories as to how to avoid flare-ups and relieve the pain. However, there is medical research being performed regularly to try to deal with these issues. Granted, you could keep a direct eye on the medical literature, but you'd rather keep an eye on the reporting of what the medical literature is finding, as you're not qualified to understand most of the literature directly. So, off to Google you go.

After a few months of trying to remember to redo your search to see if there is anything new to be read, you're told that setting up a Google Alert would be a much better way of getting the information you need. So, let's take a look at

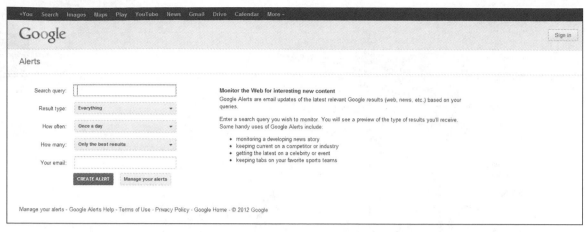

Figure 11.1 A blank Google Alert form

how to set up a Google Alert. (It is important to note that in order for Alerts to work, you must ultimately create and sign in to a Google account.)

Figure 11.1 shows the form you'll see when you get there. Here you have the following fields to fill in and options to choose from:

- *Search query*
  Enter your search terms here. In this field you can use any of the available operators that Google search makes available (Boolean, parenthesis, quotes, etc.).

- *Result type*
  Here you must choose one of the six available options: Everything, News, Blogs, Video, Discussion, Books. Choosing "Everything" performs the same sort of search as you would on the Google home page, while the others perform your search against the relevant specific search, each of which was covered elsewhere in this book.

- *How often*
  Here you specify how often you wish to receive results: As-it-happens, Once a day, or Once a week. Depending on your search query, you may wish to come back later and adjust the frequency of your results. For example, choosing "As-it-happens" might end up sending you results too fast for you to be able to read. (See also the "Deliver to" option below for additional details on this option.)

- *How many*
  Here you can choose to receive "Only the best results" or "All results." The difference between these two options may be a bit subjective and

will influence how may results you are actually presented with. In Michael's gout example, he's chosen to receive only the "best" results, while in other cases where he's looking to find every mention of a particular yet uncommon phrase, "all" is the better choice.

- *Deliver to*

   Lastly, you can choose which of your entered e-mail addresses will receive the results. You will receive one e-mail based on the schedule set in the "How often" field.

Figure 11.2 shows how to set up your gout search.

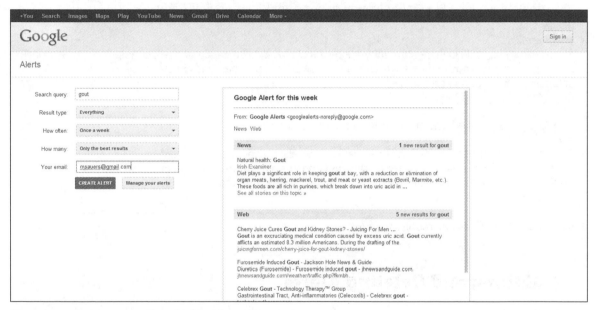

Figure 11.2 Setting up a Google Alert for *gout*

In this example a Google Alert has been set up for news items containing the keyword *gout* to be delivered once a week via e-mail.

Once you've got your form filled in as you'd like it, just click the "Create Alert" button to get things set up.

Receiving Results

Once you've got your alert set up, you'll need to sit back for a bit (especially depending on the commonality of your search terms and your delivery timeframe) and wait for your results to start coming in. In the meantime, here's an example e-mail from the gout alert (figure 11.3).

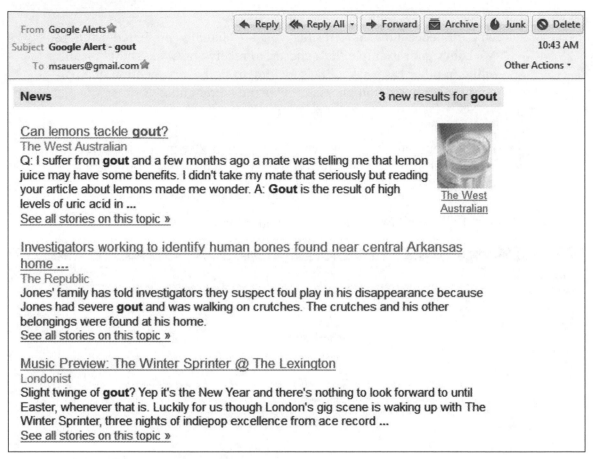

From Google Alerts 🌟

Subject **Google Alert - gout**

To msauers@gmail.com 🌟

↩ Reply   ◀◀ Reply All ▾   ➡ Forward   🗄 Archive   🍷 Junk   🚫 Delete

10:43 AM

Other Actions ▾

News   **3 new results for gout**

Can lemons tackle **gout**?
The West Australian
Q: I suffer from **gout** and a few months ago a mate was telling me that lemon
juice may have some benefits. I didn't take my mate that seriously but reading
your article about lemons made me wonder. A: **Gout** is the result of high
levels of uric acid in ...
See all stories on this topic »

The West
Australian

Investigators working to identify human bones found near central Arkansas
home ...
The Republic
Jones' family has told investigators they suspect foul play in his disappearance because
Jones had severe **gout** and was walking on crutches. The crutches and his other
belongings were found at his home.
See all stories on this topic »

Music Preview: The Winter Sprinter @ The Lexington
Londonist
Slight twinge of **gout**? Yep it's the New Year and there's nothing to look forward to until
Easter, whenever that is. Luckily for us though London's gig scene is waking up with The
Winter Sprinter, three nights of indiepop excellence from ace record ...
See all stories on this topic »

Figure 11.3 Example e-mail results for *gout*

Editing and Deleting Alerts

Let's now say that it's another few months down the line, and you decide that
you'd rather get your gout alerts more often because there's some promising
news coming in fast and furiously about a possible cure. Or, you stop working at the library and no longer need to track online mentions of your former
employer. In this case you'll need to edit and/or delete one of your alerts.

To do this, head back to the Google Alerts page and click the "Manage your
alerts" button. The next screen will show you a list of all your currently active
alerts (figure 11.4).

On this page, each of your active alerts is displayed in four columns. The
first contains your search terms, which are hyperlinked to perform the actual
search. The next column, labeled "Volume," is the type of results you're set
to receive. Column three, "How often," is the frequency of the results delivery. And the last column, "Deliver to," displays the delivery method. To edit
or delete an alert, click the appropriate "Edit" button to the far right. Once

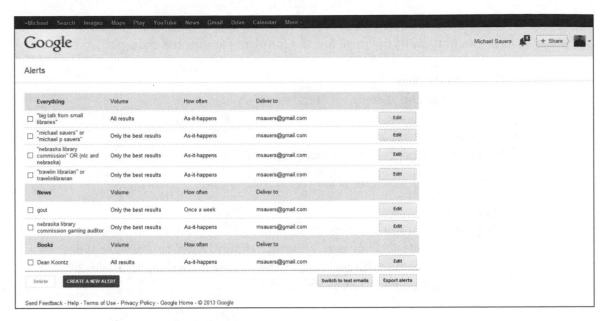

Figure 11.4 The Manage Your Alerts page

you've done that, the page will refresh giving you the ability to edit the alert (figure 11.5). Once you've made your changes, click the "Save" button to commit the changes or the "Cancel" button to prevent the changes.

To delete an alert, check the box to the left of the alert and click the "Delete" button at the bottom of the page.

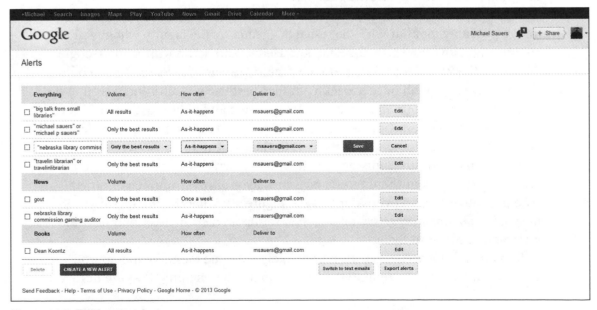

Figure 11.5 Editing an alert

Also at the bottom of the page are the following additional buttons:

- *Create a new alert*
  Takes you to the "Create an alert" page.

- *Switch to text e-mails*
  By default, Google Alert e-mails are HTML-based. If you prefer to receive text-only e-mails, click this button.

- *Export alerts*
  Clicking this button initiates the download of an alerts.csv file that contains the details of your active alerts. (Honestly, we're not sure what you would then do with this file, as there doesn't seem to be an import function for Google Alerts.)

Using Google Alerts at the Reference Desk

We'll readily admit that the two examples that we used in this chapter thus far are pretty personal to a specific person or to a small group of individuals. And we can assume that you've probably already thought of a search or two that you could set up for yourself. But you may be wondering: just how could this be used in a wider library context, from a reference desk perspective? Well, let's take a look at the following scenario.

Maybe you're the business librarian on a university campus. In this case you're probably familiar with the research agendas of the faculty whom you're supporting. How about taking that knowledge and setting up some Google Alerts for the keywords related to your faculty's areas of research? You could then receive an e-mail once a week with the "best" new results and pass those links on to the appropriate faculty member. You could either just forward the e-mail as it came from Google, or edit the content based on your knowledge and take the credit for assisting them with their research.

Now don't think that this applies just to academic situations. In a public library, take a look at the interests of your mayor or other municipal officials who may have control over your budget. Figure out what they're interested in or what problems they're trying to solve, set up an alert or two, and pass the information along to them.

In both of these scenarios, it's highly likely—if done tactfully and appropriately—that you at least remind the folks whom you're helping that the library is here to assist them. Best case, they end up thinking of you and the library whenever they need help in the future.

So, do a little research and see how Google Alerts can help you help others.

chapter 12

Google Search Tips and Tricks

THROUGHOUT THIS BOOK we've focused mainly on how to perform searches, interpret the results, and filter those results to find what you're looking for. Though we've used plenty of different examples for those searches, we haven't focused on specific content short of the broad categories of content, such as videos versus news.

However, there are some specific types of information that Google is very good at providing—not just links to sites that have your answer, but to the answers themselves. Also, even though we've focused on English-language results in this book, there are ways with Google to expand your search to more than one language for results.

In this final chapter, we present many of these options and let you know just how to take advantage of them.

Google Search Features

Beyond the advanced search features and additional database searches that Google makes available, Google provides many built-in shortcuts via web search, known as "search features." Below are the vast majority of the ones that were available at the time of this writing.

GOOGLE KNOWS MATH

Just type in a mathematical formula and you'll get your answer, as shown in figure 12.1. Enter a formula that results in a graph and you'll get the graph too, sometimes in three dimensions (figures 12.2 and 12.3).

Figure 12.1 Results for *(10*56)/2*

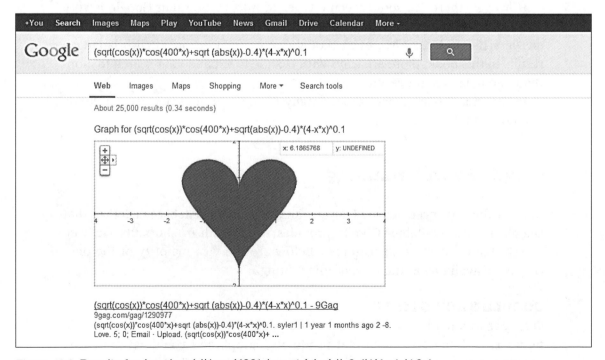

Figure 12.2 Results for *(sqrt(cos(x))*cos(400*x)+sqrt (abs(x))-0.4)*(4-x*x)^0.1*

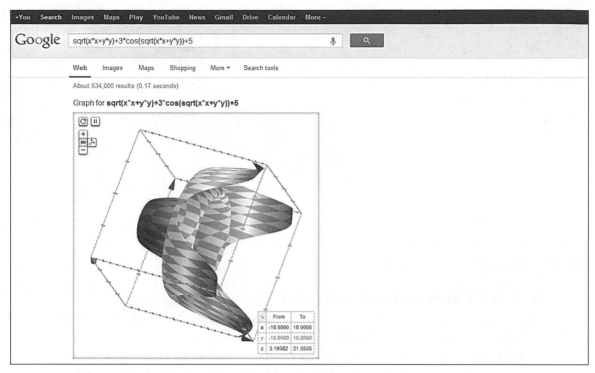

Figure 12.3 Results for *sqrt(x*x+y*y)+3*cos(sqrt(x*x+y*y))+5*

What makes this feature even better is that, as the previous two screenshots show, the results page also presents an on-screen graphing calculator you can use to do additional calculations. If you'd like to get to the calculator without first having to type in a formula, you can just enter *calculator* in the Google search field (figure 12.4).

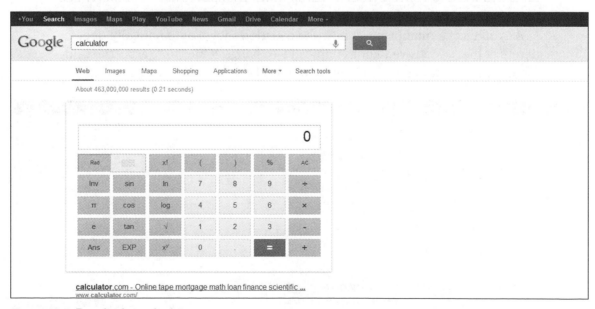

Figure 12.4 Results for *calculator*

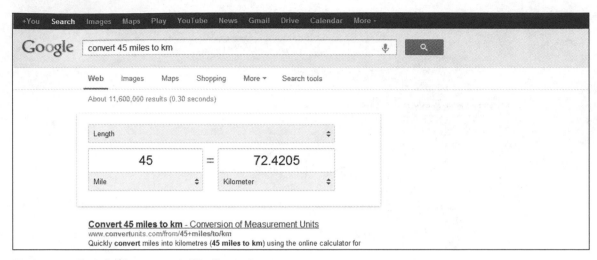

Figure 12.5 Results for *convert 45 miles to km*

GOOGLE KNOWS MEASUREMENTS

Just type in a mathematical formula or measurement conversion and you'll get your answer, as shown in figure 12.5.

Prior to the summer of 2011, asking Google to make this conversion would have just given you the answer. However, as you can see from our example, you are provided with not only the answer but also the ability to interactively change the type of conversion and the units being converted.

As you can see in figure 12.5, we've been given the answer that 45 miles is equal to 72.4205 kilometers. But what you also see is that you can enter different numbers on either side of the equation, change the unit type from the drop-down list on either side of the equation, and even change the type of units available to convert from the drop-down list above the equation (which currently states "Length") to other types of units, ranging from area to volume.

As you change numbers or units, the equation shown automatically updates to reflect the new answer. For example, if we change "Mile" to "Yard," the value for kilometer automatically changes to 0.041148, as shown in figure 12.6.

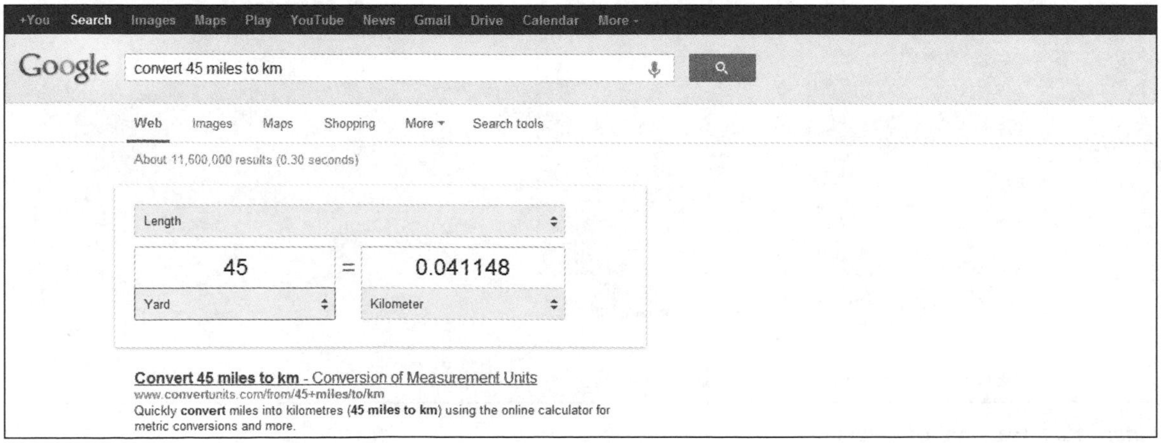

Figure 12.6 Results of changing "Mile" to "Yard"

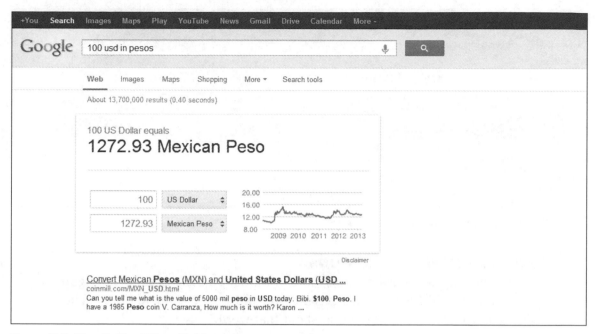

Figure 12.7 Results for *100 usd in pesos*

GOOGLE KNOWS MONEY

Need a quick currency conversion? Type in the amount and currency, then the new currency, as shown in figure 12.7.

Not only are you presented with the conversion rate, you're also presented with a graph of the exchange rate over time. Also, as with the unit conversion, there is also an interactive part to currency conversion results. From here you can change the amount in either currency and have the other one update automatically (figure 12.8).

Figure 12.8 Result of changing 100 US Dollars to 200

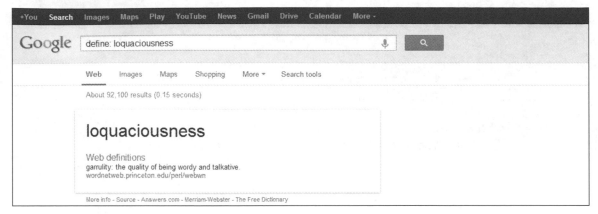

Figure 12.9 Results for *define: loquaciousness*

GOOGLE KNOWS DEFINITIONS

Simply type *define* followed by the word you want defined, as shown in figure 12.9., and you will receive both a definition and also links to additional sites that can provide more information about that word.

GOOGLE KNOWS MOVIES

Search on a movie name or just *movie* to see theater locations and showtimes in your area, as shown in figure 12.10. For each movie you'll be presented with the title (hyperlinked to additional information and show locations for that film), the film's length, rating, and genre, and a link to the trailer. Clicking the "Show more movies" link will extend the list of movies displayed (figure 12.11) and also give you a "See all movies" link, which takes you to a page with many more details and options for finding where and when your film is showing (figure 12.12).

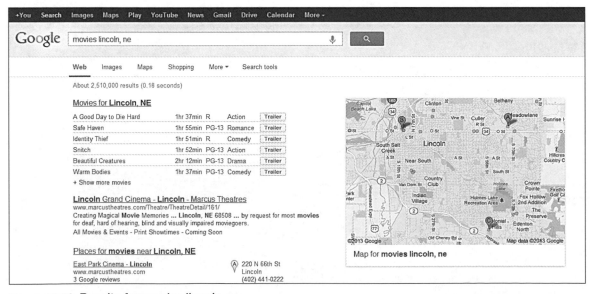

Figure 12.10 Results for *movies lincoln, ne*

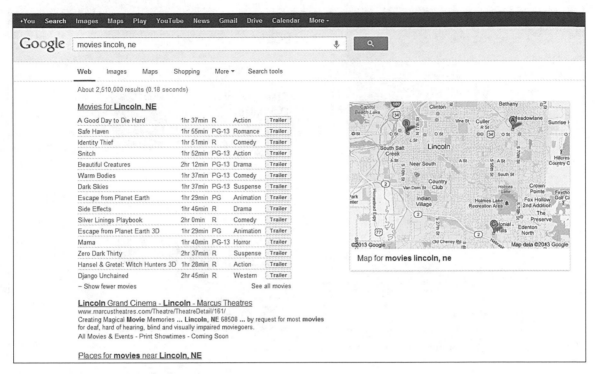

Figure 12.11 Results of clicking "Show more movies"

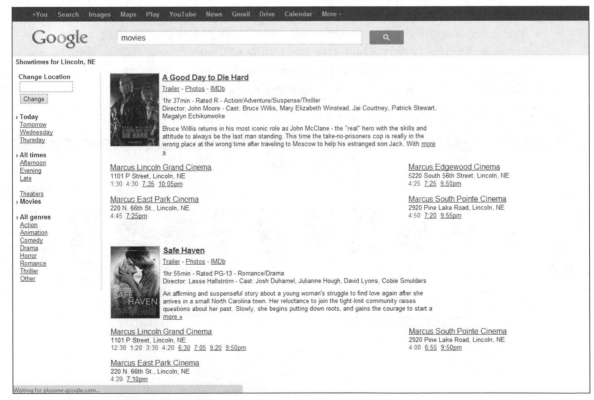

Figure 12.12 Results of clicking "See all movies"

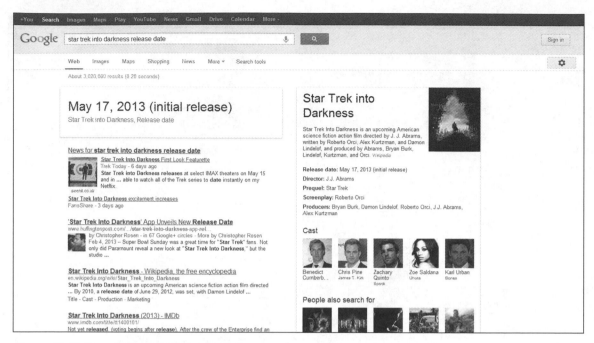

Figure 12.13 Results for *star trek into darkness release date*

To find out when a movie will be in the theaters, search on the movie name with the phrase "release date" (figure 12.13). This will also work for video games.

For a list of movies that an actor has been in, search on the actor's name and *movies* (figure 12.14). The top of the results will appear as a side-scrolling list of the movies—with their DVD covers serving as links to a new search on the movie itself—while still maintaining the original list of the actor' movies above the search results.

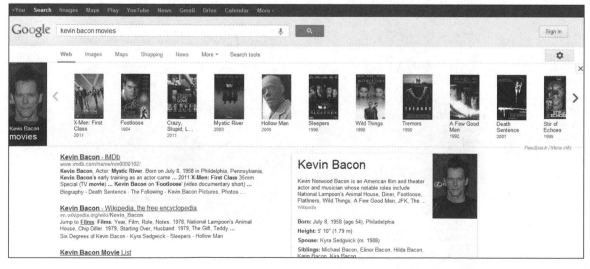

Figure 12.14 Results for *kevin bacon movies*

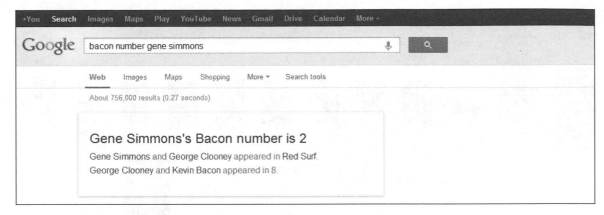

Figure 12.15 Results for *bacon number gene simmons*

Speaking of Kevin Bacon, have you ever played Six Degrees of Kevin Bacon? It's a game based on the fact that Kevin Bacon has been in so many movies that you can link any actor through their film roles to him within six steps. The result is called the actor's Bacon Number. In 2012, Google added the Bacon Number search tool—search for any actor with the phrase "Bacon Number" and it will automatically calculate the actor's number, showing you the connections between them and Kevin Bacon (figure 12.15).

GOOGLE KNOWS MUSIC

As with actors and movies, for a list of albums that a band or musician has released, search on the band's or musician's name and *albums* (figure 12.16). The top of the results will appear as a side-scrolling list of the albums, with their covers serving as links to a new search on the album itself—again, while still maintaining the original list of the band's albums above the search results.

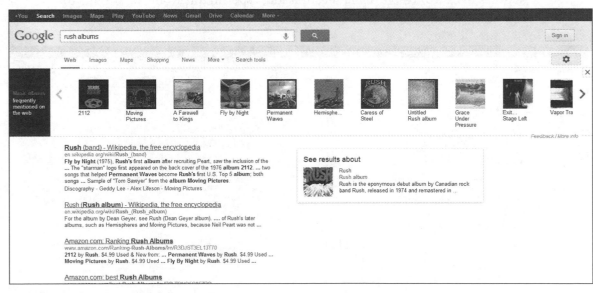

Figure 12.16 Results for *rush albums*

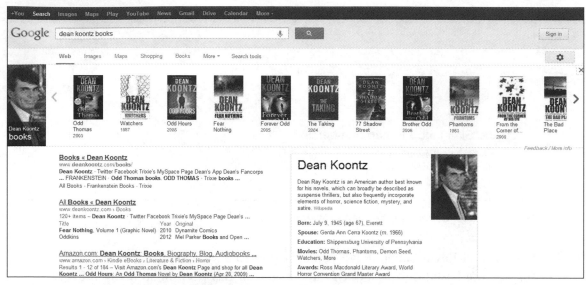

Figure 12.17 Results for *dean koontz books*

GOOGLE KNOWS AUTHORS

And of course, for a list of books that an author has written, search on the author's name and *books* (figure 12.17). The top of the results will appear as a side-scrolling list of the books, with their covers serving as links to a new search on the book itself, while still maintaining the original list of the author's books above the search results.

GOOGLE KNOWS FLIGHTS

View live arrival and departure information for U.S. flights just by searching the name of the airline and the flight number (figure 12.18). To see flight schedules to or from a particular destination, type "flights from" or "flights to" followed by the city or airport of interest (figure 12.19).

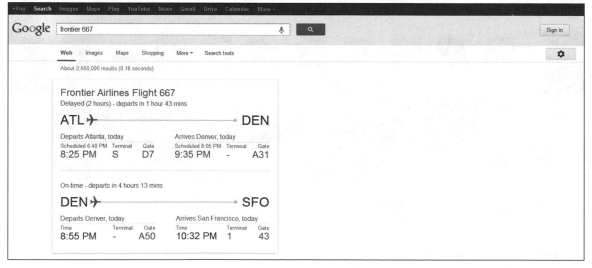

Figure 12.18 Results for *frontier 667*

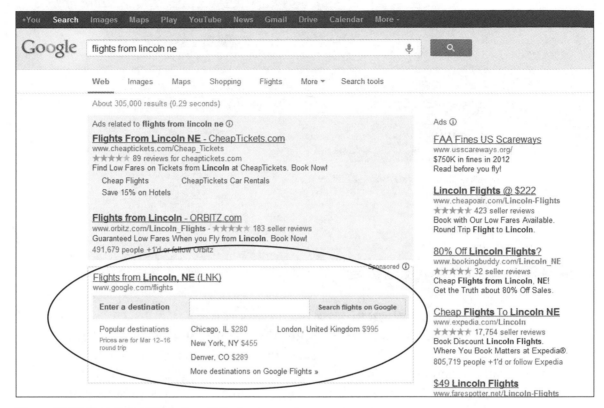

Figure 12.19 Result for *flights from lincoln, ne*

GOOGLE KNOWS NUMBERS

Google can automatically recognize several types of numbers. These include UPS (United Parcel Service), FedEx, and USPS (United States Postal Service) tracking numbers (figure 12.20), as well as VINs (vehicle identification numbers) and UPCs (Universal Product Codes) (figure 12.21). Just type any of these into Google to get a link to the results you need.

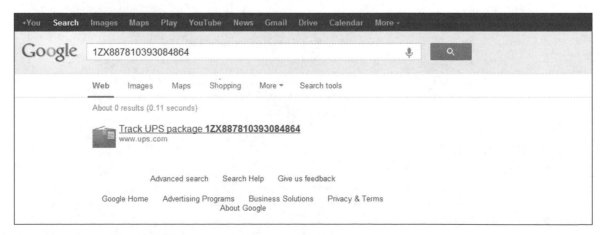

Figure 12.20 Results for package *1ZX887810393084864*

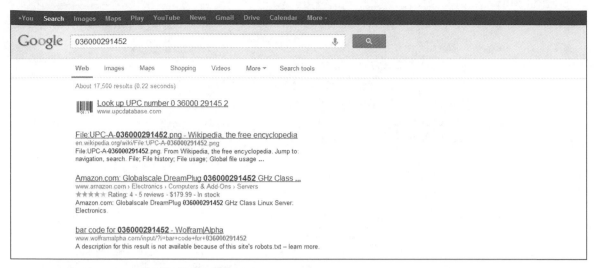

Figure 12.21 Results for UPC *036000291452*

GOOGLE KNOWS STOCKS

Looking for information on your favorite stock? Enter the ticker symbol and you'll get back the name of the company, the current stock price, a graph of recent values, and other information, such as the most recent open, high, and low prices (figure 12.22). You'll also be presented with links to sites with additional information such as Google Finance (figure 12.23), CNN Money, and Reuters.

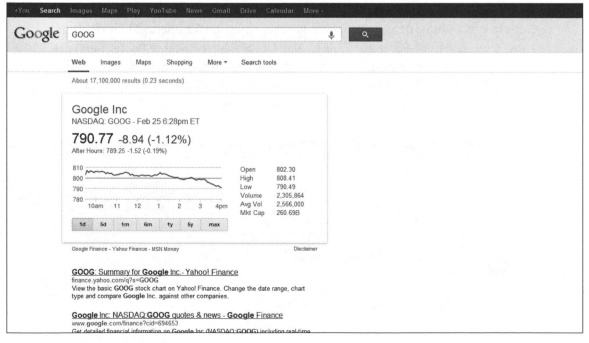

Figure 12.22 Results for *GOOG*

Figure 12.23 The Google Finance page for *GOOG*

GOOGLE KNOWS THE WEATHER

Start your search with the word *weather* followed by a city and state or zip code to receive the current and forecasted weather for that area (figure 12.24). You'll also be provided with links to pages with additional information such as the Weather Channel, Weather Underground, and AccuWeather.

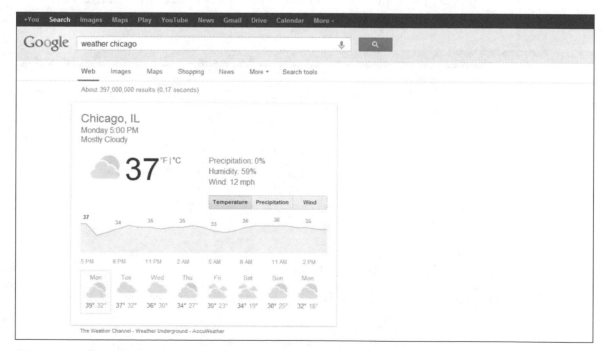

Figure 12.24 Results for *weather chicago*

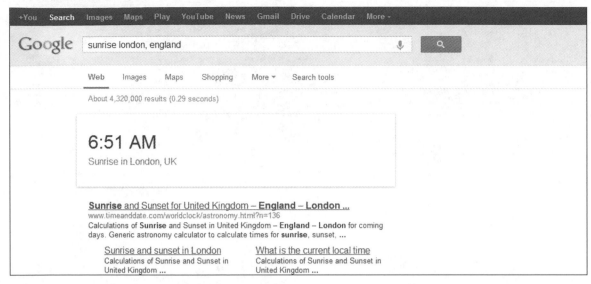

Figure 12.25 Results for *sunrise london, england*

GOOGLE KNOWS SUNRISE AND SUNSET

If you're wondering when the sun is going to rise or set, just ask Google. If you omit the location, Google will attempt to figure out where you are and give you the time for that location (figure 12.25).

GOOGLE KNOWS THE TIME

What time it is in San Francisco? Enter *time* and the location to find out (figure 12.26).

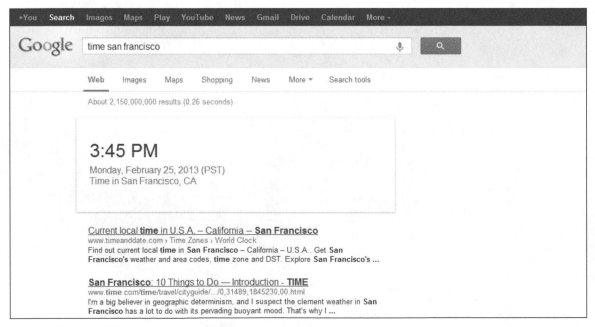

Figure 12.26 Results for *time san francisco*

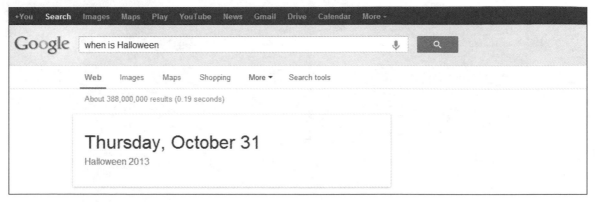

Figure 12.27 Results for *when is Halloween*

GOOGLE KNOWS HOLIDAYS

When you want to know the day or date of a particular holiday, just ask Google. For example, let's say that you want to know what day of the week Halloween falls on this year. Just search for *when is halloween*; at the top of the search results, you'll see the answer (figure 12.27). You can also search for some of those more obscure holidays, like National Mole Day. Note that many holidays are region-specific, so you may see different holidays depending on your location settings.

GOOGLE KNOWS THE SCORE

Wondering what the score was of your favorite team's last game or when their next game is scheduled? Just enter the name of your team to find out (figure 12.28). If the game is currently on, you'll be provided with the most current statistics available. If you're interested in seeing more of a team's upcoming schedule, just click the " + Show more games" link.

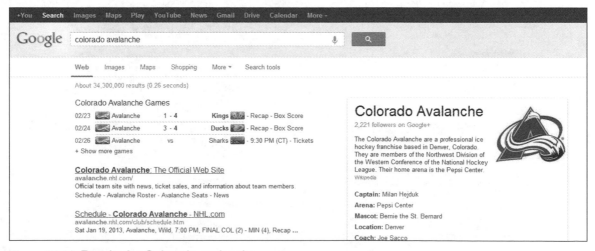

Figure 12.28 Results for *Colorado avalanche*

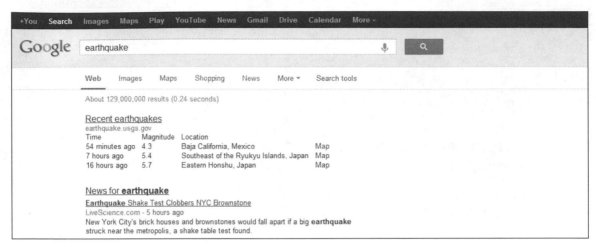

Figure 12.29 Results for *earthquake*

GOOGLE KNOWS WHEN THE GROUND SHAKES

Heard about a recent earthquake somewhere in the world and want to know more? Type in *earthquake* and a location to get the data you're looking for. For information on recent quakes, don't specify a location (figure 12.29).

GOOGLE KNOWS PUBLIC DATA

Google has access to an immense amount of public data—so much that we couldn't possibly cover it all here. But as just one example, enter *population* and a location. This provides you with the current population figure, that figure's date and source, and a graph of the population change over time (figure 12.30).

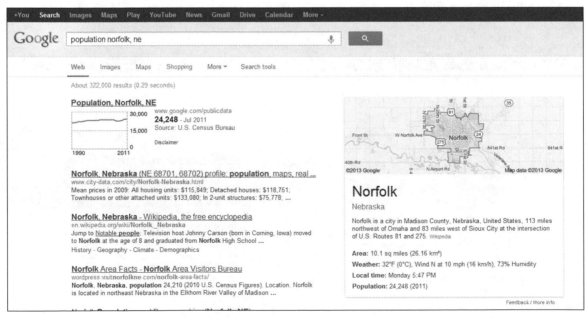

Figure 12.30 Results for *population norfolk, ne*

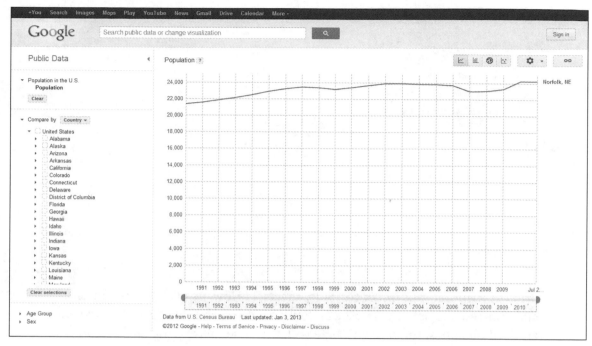

Figure 12.31 Additional details view for *population norfolk, ne*

Additionally, if you click on the graph, you'll be taken to another page with even more detailed data and plenty of options for customizing the graph with additional information (figure 12.31).

GOOGLE KNOWS MALADIES AND MEDICATIONS

Have some medications that you're researching? When you search on the name of a medication, Google gives you the brand and chemical names, a

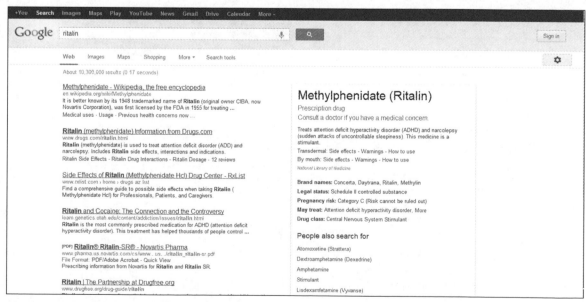

Figure 12.32 Results for *ritalin*

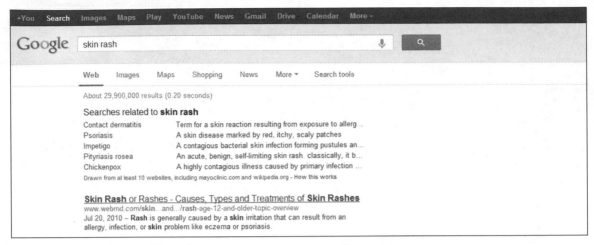

Figure 12.33 Results for *skin rash*

brief description, and links to "Side effects," "How to take," "Precautions," and "Missed a dose" (figure 12.32). You can also search for diseases and generalized maladies, for which Google will return details and/or further options (figure 12.33).

GOOGLE KNOWS FOOD

If you're looking for nutritional information for basic foods try doing a simple search on the name of that food. Searches for natural foods like apples, grapes,

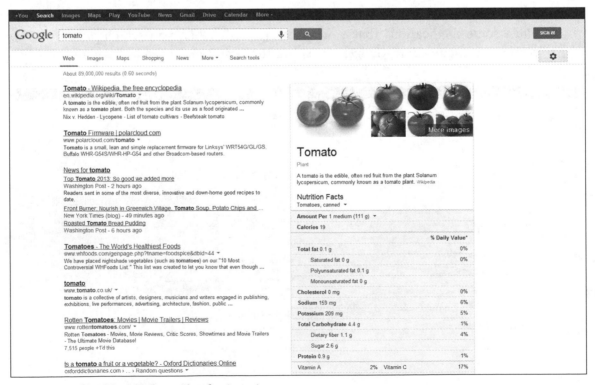

Figure 12.34 Nutritional information for *tomato*

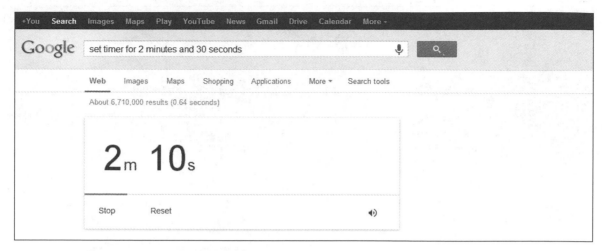

Figure 12.35 Google counting down time from 2 minutes and 30 seconds

and tomatoes will result in nutritional data appearing to the right of the Web search results, as shown in figure 12.34. Google is adding more foods all the time so something that receives no similar results now may do so in the future. However, don't expect to get detailed nutritional information for prepackaged foods for the foreseeable future.

GOOGLE KNOWS WHEN TO STOP

Need a simple countdown? Just tell Google to set timer for and then enter the length of time you need. At the top of your search results (figure 12.35) you'll see a live countdown timer along with a blue line that fills in as the time runs out, stop and restart links, and a speaker icon to turn off the audible alert that will occur when time runs out. When the time does run out, the stop link will turn into an OK link, which you'll need to click to turn off the alarm.

GOOGLE KNOWS WHERE TO BEGIN

Google has a little-known separate Web site titled "What do you love?" (http://www.wdyl.com). Head over there and you'll be asked to answer the question "What do you love?" (figure 12.36). In this case, instead of receiving specific

Figure 12.36 The What Do You Love home page

Figure 12.37 The *I love libraries* results page

results from a specific type of Google search, you'll be presented with a long page of both results and links to further searches from across many Google services. For example, a search here for libraries (figure 12.37) returns results ranging from "Latest news about libraries" (Google News), "Start a libraries discussion group" (Google Groups), "Scour the Earth for libraries" (Google Earth), "Explore libraries in #d" (Google SketchUp), "Measure popularity of libraries on the web" (Google Trends), "See pictures of libraries" (Google Images), and many more. Results do vary significantly (for example, searching for an author's name offers the ability to find patents about that author), but if you've got a patron who doesn't know where to start on a somewhat broad topic, this can be a great way to get them to think about just what type of resources they're looking for.

Google Translate

Although Google Translate isn't a way to perform a search, it can still come in handy when dealing with search results that appear in a language that you don't read. Granted, if you're using English keywords, chances are you'll get back only English-language pages. However, searches for things such as place names or events that happen in the non-English-speaking world are more likely to return foreign-language results. This is where Google Translate comes into play.

There are four ways that you can take advantage of Google Translate: three that are browser neutral, and one that's specific to Google Chrome. Google can translate text, translate a web page, translate a document, and (Chrome only) give you an on-the-fly translation. Let's take a brief look at each operation.

The first three are all available by going to the Google Translate page at http://translate.google.com (figure 12.38). Here you'll find two boxes, one for the original text on the left and the translated text on the right. To translate a block of text, all you need to do is type or paste it into the box on the left and click the blue "Translate" button. By default, Google automatically detects the

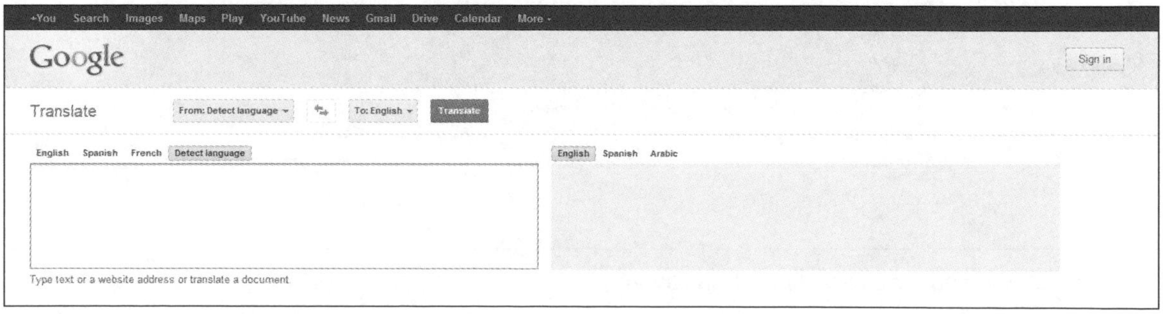

Figure 12.38 Google Translate

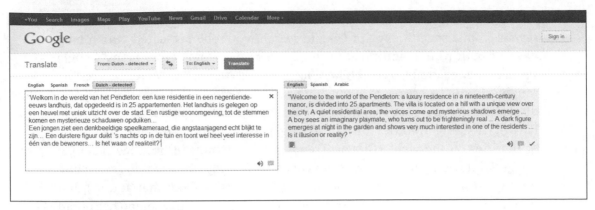

Figure 12.39 Results of translating some text

original language and translates it into your default language, based on your location (for us, that would be English) then displays the translation in the box on the right (figure 12.39). If either of those assumptions is incorrect, you can use the "From:" and "To:" buttons above the translation boxes to change either or both of the languages (figure 12.40).

If instead you have the URL of a web page you wish to translate, you can enter the URL in the box on the left and click the link displayed in the right box. In this case, the page will be loaded and displayed as if you had gone directly to that page, but it has been translated into the language you chose. Figure 12.41 shows an example of a page originally in German, translated into English. In this display you'll also have drop-down lists to change the "From:"

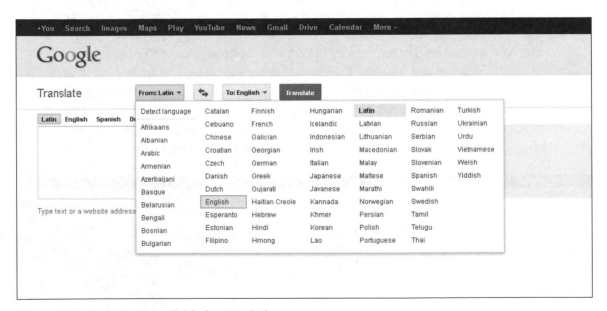

Figure 12.40 Languages available for translation

Figure 12.41 Result of translating the German-language Wikipedia home page into English

and "To:" languages, along with buttons to switch between the original and translated versions of the page.

If you find yourself with an electronic document such as a Word file that you need to translate, find the "translate a document" link beneath the box on the left. Clicking this link takes you to another page (figure 12.42), where you can browse for and upload a document to Google for translation. Figure 12.43 shows an example result of this process.

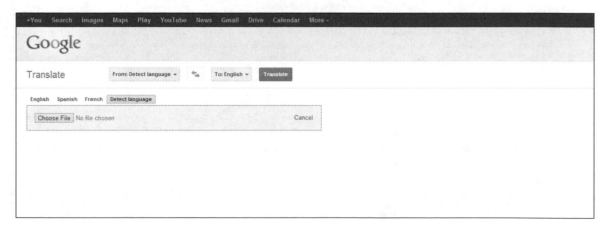

Figure 12.42 Google Translate document upload page

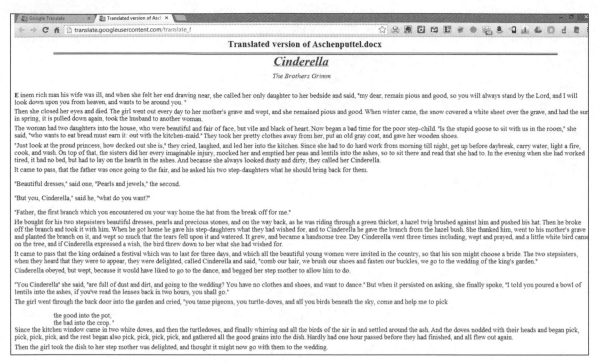

Figure 12.43 Result of translating an uploaded Word document

Lastly, if you're a user of the Google Chrome browser, the web page translation feature is actually built in. As shown in figure 12.44 when you go to the Italian Wikipedia home page, a toolbar appears at the top of the page that

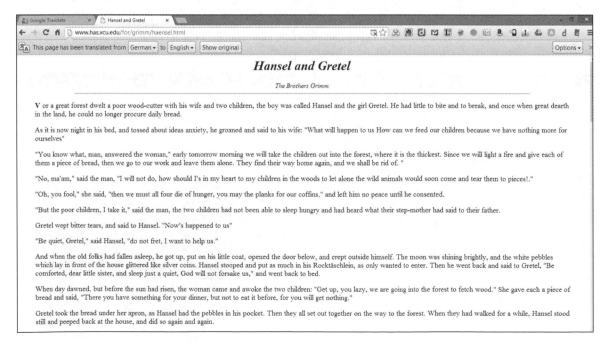

Figure 12.44 Chrome translation interface

states, "This page is in Italian. Would you like to translate it?" Here you can choose a different source language (should Google have gotten that wrong) and then choose either to "Translate" the page or to decline the translation by clicking the "Nope" button. If you do choose to translate, as you continue to surf, Chrome will continue to translate until you tell it to stop.

If you use this feature regularly, you may want to explore the "Options" button off to the right of the translation bar. You can instruct Chrome to always translate pages in a particular language, never translate pages from that language, or never to translate pages from the current site.

Granted, Google's translation service may not be as good as hiring a professional, but we can say from experience that it's been good enough every time we've needed it.

index